Real prayer

CONNECTING WITH OUR HEAVENLY FATHER

by Anne Woodcock

Real prayer
The Good Book Guide to Real prayer
© The Good Book Company, 2016. Reprinted 2017, 2020.
Series Conultants: Tim Chester, Tim Thornborough, Carl Laferton, Anne Woodcock

Published by:
The Good Book Company

thegoodbook.com | www.thegoodbook.co.uk
thegoodbook.com.au | thegoodbook.co.nz | thegoodbook.co.in

ISBN: 9781910307595 | Printed in Turkey

Design by André Parker

CONTENTS

Introduction: Good Book Guides

Every Bible-study group is different—yours may take place in a church building, in a home or in a cafe, on a train, over a leisurely mid-morning coffee or squashed into a 30-minute lunch break. Your group may include new Christians, mature Christians, non-Christians, mums and tots, students, businessmen or teens. That's why we've designed these *Good Book Guides* to be flexible for use in many different situations.

Our aim in each session is to uncover the meaning of a passage, and see how it fits into the "big picture" of the Bible. But that can never be the end. We also need to appropriately apply what we have discovered to our lives. Let's take a look at what is included:

⊕ **Talkabout:** Most groups need to "break the ice" at the beginning of a session, and here's the question that will do that. It's designed to get people talking around a subject that will be covered in the course of the Bible study.

⊕ **Investigate:** The Bible text for each session is broken up into manageable chunks, with questions that aim to help you understand what the passage is about. **The Leader's Guide** contains **guidance on questions**, and sometimes ⊗ additional "follow-up" questions.

☺ **Explore more (optional):** These questions will help you connect what you have learned to other parts of the Bible, so you can begin to fit it all together like a jig-saw; or occasionally look at a part of the passage that's not dealt with in detail in the main study.

➔ **Apply:** As you go through a Bible study, you'll keep coming across **apply** sections. These are questions to get the group discussing what the Bible teaching means in practice for you and your church. ☺ **Getting personal** is an opportunity for you to think, plan and pray about the changes that you personally may need to make as a result of what you have learned.

⬆ **Pray:** We want to encourage prayer that is rooted in God's word—in line with His concerns, purposes and promises. So each session ends with an opportunity to review the truths and challenges highlighted by the Bible study, and turn them into prayers of request and thanksgiving.

The **Leader's Guide** and introduction provide historical background information, explanations of the Bible texts for each session, ideas for **optional extra** activities, and guidance on how best to help people uncover the truths of God's word.

Why study *Real prayer*?

What does the word "prayer" make you think of? For many, it's a religious activity for old people and vicars. Or a weird superstitious ritual. Or something they've done in a moment of desperation. For Christians, the word often conjures up a heavy sense of duty—something we ought, and struggle, to do.

"Prayer" is one of those words that can make us cringe inwardly. Perhaps we feel confusion because we don't really understand what prayer is or how it works. Or we feel frustration because great things that people promise will happen when we pray never materialise. Or we feel guilt, because actually we do have some idea of what prayer is and why we should do it, but we still don't!

Yet despite the confusion and mixed feelings, at one time or another just about everyone prays. Millions worldwide do it habitually or devotedly, every day. And in moments of terror, even atheists may cry out to the God they don't believe in. We're humans, so we pray—but often as though we're shooting in the dark.

Wonderfully, the Bible—and Jesus especially—shows us what real prayer is: why and how we can talk to the real, living God with humble confidence, knowing that he will hear and answer.

That's not true of all or even most of what is claimed to be prayer in our world. Some prayer is not really about talking; some is not talking to the real living God; and some is done in a way that God will not respond to. It's only through Jesus Christ that we can "connect" with God.

This Good Book Guide looks at what the Christian message tells us about how and why we can talk to God knowing that he will listen and respond. Forget formulas and techniques. This is about real communication with the real God—the unique Christian privilege of real prayer.

1

Luke 18 v 9-14
WHY PRAY?

⊕ talkabout

1. How do you answer the question: why pray?

⊥ investigate

The Bible says a lot about prayer, but—surprisingly perhaps—it doesn't specifically answer the question: why pray? And although the Bible assumes that it is important and right for people to pray to God, it also highlights a fundamental problem with our prayers to God: "Your iniquities have separated you from your God; your sins have hidden his face from you, so that he will not hear" (Isaiah 59 v 2).

Jesus' story of two men in the Jerusalem Temple, contrasting a prayer that God won't listen to with a prayer that he wonderfully answers, reveals the first and foundational reason for why we should pray to God, and the kind of prayer that will connect us with him.

▶ Read Luke 18 v 9-14

2. The two men in Jesus' story—the Pharisee and the tax collector—are based on real people that Jesus has already met in Luke's Gospel. What do the following passages reveal about Pharisees, tax collectors, and Jesus? (Complete the table on the next page.)

> **DICTIONARY**
>
> **Righteousness (v 9):** goodness; being right in God's eyes.
> **Parable (v 9):** a simple story with a deeper meaning.
> **Pharisee (v 10):** member of a religious group that was very strict about Jewish law.
> **Tax collector (v 10):** a deeply despised job that involved collaborating with the Roman occupiers of Israel, and cheating taxpayers.
> **Justified (v 14):** given a verdict of "not guilty".

	PHARISEES	TAX COLLECTORS	JESUS
Luke 15 v 1-7			
Luke 16 v 13-15		✕	

3. Contrast the two men in Jesus' parable. Think about:
• their way of life.

• their posture in the temple.

• what they pray about or for.

• The Pharisee isn't lying when he says, "I am not like ... this tax collector", so what's the problem with saying this?

4. The Pharisee's prayer begins, "God, I thank you..." but look at his next sentence (v 12). What is the real focus of this prayer?

• What, then, would you say is the real purpose of his prayer?

Alternative translations of the beginning of verse 11 are: "The Pharisee ... prayed thus with himself" (NKJV) or "... prayed to himself" (ESV footnotes). The effect of the Pharisee's prayer is that he doesn't speak to God at all!

5. Compare the tax collector's prayer. How is it opposite to the Pharisee's prayer?

• How does Jesus show that this kind of prayer "works"?

6. Why does Jesus tell this story (v 9)?

• What is his message to these people (and us)?

7. From this story, especially verse 14, how do you think Jesus would answer the question: Why pray?

• How would he answer the question: What kind of prayer moves God to act?

⊡ apply

It's possible to think that we're praying, and yet that might be so far from talking to the real God based on the reality of who he is and what we are like that it isn't real prayer at all!

8. What antidote to this have we seen (see question 2, 15 v 1), and how can we encourage this antidote in our own lives and churches?

Unlike the tax collector, many—because of shame and guilt—don't pray when in fact they can and should.

9. What antidote to this have we seen (see question 2, 15 v 3-7), and how can we encourage this antidote in our own lives and churches?

⊡ getting personal

Who do you most often resemble—the Pharisee or the tax collector? Think through these questions:

How often do you confess sin?

How much of your praying involves thanking God for what he has done for you?

How often do you go without praying at all?

If your first two answers are "not much" and your last one is "quite a lot", chances are that you are still struggling with your "inner Pharisee".

Take time right now to pray the tax collector's prayer and think about Jesus' words in 18 v 14.

⊡ explore more

optional

In Athens Paul proclaimed the truth about God to people who knew nothing about him. Although the word "prayer" is not mentioned, Paul speaks about seeking, reaching out for and finding God.

> **Read Acts 17 v 22-31**

What reasons for why we should pray can you work out from what Paul says here? (See v 25, 27, 30 and 31.)

What here should humble us, and what should encourage us to pray?

Imagine someone asks you to explain prayer. Use this passage to explain why humbly asking God for mercy is the only way to truly pray.

⬇ investigate

10. Followers of Jesus have now received God's mercy in Christ. So why do we need to keep praying? Find reasons from the following passages:

• Luke 21 v 34-36

• Romans 15 v 30-32

• 1 Timothy 2 v 1-4

• How do these reasons to keep praying underline the lessons of Jesus' parable in Luke 18?

➡ apply

11. Write down the last three things you have prayed for. If your prayers rarely reflect the themes highlighted in Q10, why do you think that might be?

⊡ getting personal

Write down something you hope to learn about prayer in this Bible-study series, or some way in which you hope your praying will change.

↥ pray

Learn from the error of the Pharisee. How have you talked yourself up and done down others? How do you need to humble yourself? Take time now to confess these things to God.

Learn from the tax collector. What things do you need God's mercy for? Spend time asking God for these things.

2 Matthew 6 v 5-8
TO THE FATHER: HOW NOT TO PRAY

The story so far

Real prayer starts with sinners humbly asking God for mercy; and God answers by justifiying them in Jesus Christ.

⊕ talkabout

1. List some of the privileges and joys of a good father/child relationship. You could compare this relationship with that of a boss and employee.

⊕ investigate

In this session and the next, we will look at what Jesus taught about prayer in the Sermon on the Mount (recorded in Matthew's Gospel, chapters 5 to 7).

2. **Read Matthew 5 v 1-2.** Who is Jesus particularly speaking to in the Sermon on the Mount?

• Why is it important to be clear about this, do you think?

> **Read Matthew 6 v 5-8**

3. How does Jesus choose to describe God's relationship with Jesus' followers in these verses?

DICTIONARY

Hypocrites (v 5): people who look good outwardly but are very different inwardly.
Synagogues (v 5): where Jews met to worship God and learn from the Scriptures.
Pagans (v 7): those who worship gods other than the one true God.

• This view of God is unique to the Bible. What does it say about God? And what does it say about us?

4. How do hypocrites pray (v 5)?

• Why do they pray like that?

5. What is Jesus' antidote here to hypocritical prayer (v 6)?

6. What truth about God does Jesus highlight to expose the hypocrites' wrong thinking (v 6)?

• How will this encourage us to pray to God privately?

⮕ apply

7. We may find it hard to spend time praying when no one else knows we are doing that except God. When we don't pray privately, how does it reveal our wrong view...

• of God?

• of the purpose and value of prayer?

• When we pray like the hypocrites, what are we depending on to feel good about ourselves and to impress God?

🙂 getting personal

Jesus is not against praying in public—after all, he did that himself (e.g. Luke 9 v 16; 10 v 21-23; 22 v 39-41; John 17). But he warns against the hypocrisy of only praying in front of others, and never really talking to God.

How much do you pray in private?

What have you learned from Jesus to help you stop praying to impress others and to start really talking to God?

⊌ investigate

8. How do pagans pray (Matthew 6 v 7)?

- Why do they pray like that?

9. What truth about God does Jesus highlight that will encourage his followers to pray differently from the pagans (v 8)?

- How does Jesus want us to pray, do you think, based on understanding this truth about God?

10. If our Father knows all our needs before we even ask him (v 8), what is the purpose of praying to him about these things, do you think? (Look at Paul's experience in 2 Corinthians 1 v 8-11).

⊡ explore more

optional

Luke 11 v 1-13 also records some of Jesus' teaching about prayer from the Sermon on the Mount, along with this parable about prayer.

> ❯ **Read Luke 11 v 5-13**

Why did the man in the parable get the bread that he needed (v 8)?

What's the difference between the friend (v 7-8) and our Father God?

Since God our Father is not like our human friends, what does Jesus say we should do, and what can we be confident of (v 9-10)?

How does Jesus show that it is illogical and unreasonable to doubt that God can and will answer our prayers (v 11-13)?

There are two things that we need to understand that will drive us to pray as Jesus taught:
(1) That we have needs that we cannot supply.
(2) That God is our heavenly Father, who meets our needs by giving good gifts when we ask him.

➔ apply

11. What pagan-type praying is popular today in your local community and culture? (Think about how people pray and how they talk about prayer.)

• Why might we sometimes find these ways of praying attractive?

- How does this study help you want to pray in a Christian way, and not in a pagan way?

12. Jesus' antidote for pagan-type praying is trust in God's perfect provision for all our needs. How can we help each other grow in this trust?

⊡ getting personal

"Your Father knows what you need before you ask him."

Why, then, would you look anywhere else to get what you need?!

⊕ pray

On your own... commit to praying privately this week to your heavenly Father. and ask for his help with this. Think about when and where you could do this. Don't be unrealistic about what you can manage, but don't miss this opportunity to put into practice Jesus' teaching on prayer.

Together... share and pray for the needs of people you know, remembering that your Father in heaven knows all these needs before you ask him.

3 Matthew 6 v 9-15
TO THE FATHER: HOW TO PRAY

The story so far

Real prayer starts with sinners humbly asking God for mercy; and God answers by justifiying them in Jesus Christ.

Our heavenly Father sees and know everything, so we mustn't pray like hypocrites and we needn't pray like pagans.

⤳ talkabout

1. What would you say about the Lord's Prayer to someone who doesn't know anything about it?

⤓ investigate

❯ Read Matthew 6 v 9-15

When Jesus says, "This, then, is how you should pray" (v 9), he doesn't mean these are the only words we ever use in prayer. Elsewhere (but not here) he also tells us to pray for those who persecute us (Matthew 5 v 44), and to ask God to give the Holy Spirit (Luke 11 v 13). So we see that the Lord's Prayer isn't simply a formula to be recited; rather, it's a pattern to help our prayers reflect God's priorities and concerns.

DICTIONARY

Hallowed (v 9): this part of the prayer asks that God will be seen to be holy.
Kingdom (v 10): all those saved from their sins by Jesus' death, reconciled with God, and living under the rule of Jesus.
Debts (v 12): here, our sins against God.
Debtors (v 12): here, those who have sinned against us.
The evil one (v 13): God's enemy—Satan, or the devil.

The requests in the Lord's Prayer can be divided into two parts: verses 9-10 focus on three great concerns of God; verses 11-13 express three great human needs.

"Our Father in heaven"

2. How does this way of addressing God show:
• that we can be confident when we pray?

• that we need to be humble when we pray?

"Hallowed be your name"

3. Read part of David's prayer in **2 Samuel 7 v 22-26**. What two things done by God for his people make his name great?

• Read **John 12 v 23-24, 27-28**. What is Jesus speaking about that will make God's name great?

• In light of these passages, what should we pray for when we ask God to hallow his name?

"Your kingdom come"

What is this request asking? To understand, it will help to look at what the New Testament teaches about God's kingdom.

- The kingdom of God comes when the gospel is preached (Luke 10 v 1, 9-11, 16); we see it when we see who Jesus is (9 v 27-29); and we enter it by becoming a follower of Jesus (18 v 18-25).

- The kingdom of God is seen when Jesus' followers live in a way that pleases God (Romans 14 v 17-18).

- The kingdom of God will come fully at the end of history when Jesus returns (Luke 21 v 27-31).

4. Now work out what it means in practice to pray, "Your kingdom come".

"Your will be done, on earth as it is in heaven"

5. From the following passages find out some of what the New Testament teaches about God's will. What, then, should Christians be praying for when we ask, "Your will be done"?

- 1 Thessalonians 4 v 3
- 1 Thessalonians 5 v 16-18
- 1 Peter 2 v 13-15

- How do you think Christians living out God's will in these areas compare with those around them?

⊡ apply

6. Look again at what we've learned in questions 3 to 5. What can we do that will most hallow God's name, promote God's kingdom and do God's will in this world?

- Write down some things you have been challenged to start praying about.

⊡ getting personal

Often we feel guilty about prayer: we know we don't do it enough, or when we do, we find it hard going. What difference does Jesus' teaching here make—what excites you about real prayer?

Perhaps you've never really prayed for God's name, God's kingdom and God's will. Why not take a break right now to do just that?

⊡ investigate

▶ **Re-read Matthew 6 v 11-15**

"Give us today our daily bread"

7. Why the focus on "today", do you think? And why only "bread"?

- What can make it difficult for us to ask like this from our heavenly Father?

"And forgive us our debts, as we also have forgiven our debtors"

Jesus is teaching his disciples (5 v 1), who have already repented and believed in him, and have received forgiveness. But Jesus' followers continue in these things (Colossians 2 v 6)—they keep repenting, trusting in him and asking for forgiveness (see also 1 John 1 v 7 and 9).

8. Jesus teaches in Matthew 6 that his disciples need to seek God's forgiveness each day. But what must we do first and why? (See also verses 14-15.)

- How do Jesus' words here fit with the Bible's teaching that we are made right with God through his grace (e.g. Ephesians 2 v 8-9), and not through anything we do?

"And lead us not into temptation, but deliver us from the evil one"

The root of the Greek word used here for "temptation" can also mean "test" or "trial" (e.g. Revelation 3 v 10). Sometimes it has a negative meaning, describing sinful behaviour towards Jesus or God (e.g. Matthew 4 v 7; 16 v 1-4; Acts 5 v 9), or a process involving the devil and/or our sinful desires that can lead people into sin (e.g. 1 Corinthians 7 v 5). Sometimes it has a positive meaning, describing endurance through difficult experiences that results in maturity and proof of the genuineness of our faith (e.g. James 1 v 12)—and for Jesus, proof of his identity: the sinless Son of God (e.g. Hebrews 4 v 15).

9. What do you think will ensure that a difficult experience leads to maturity in faith, rather than into sin of some kind?

10. There are two requests in Matthew 6 v 13: When we pray, "Lead us..." how are we being humble? And when we pray, "Deliver us..." what are we to be confident about?

⊡ apply

Humble confidence before our heavenly Father (see Q2) is the root from which real praying grows. Each request in v 9-13 shows both humble dependence on God, and confidence in him to provide what we need.

11. How do we grow in both?

⊡ getting personal

Pick out one thing you particularly need to take to heart from Jesus' brilliant model prayer.

⊡ pray

Before praying together, each share two prayer points, one reflecting something from verses 9-10, and the other from verses 11-13.

During the week think of six prayer points specific to your life that echo each of the six requests in the Lord's Prayer.

4 THROUGH THE SON: PRAYING CONFIDENTLY

The story so far

Real prayer starts with sinners humbly asking God for mercy; and God answers by justifiying them in Jesus Christ.

Our heavenly Father sees and know everything, so we mustn't pray like hypocrites and we needn't pray like pagans.

Jesus teaches that prayer to our heavenly Father is first about seeking his glory and will, and then about asking him to provide for our needs.

⊕ talkabout

1. Why do people think that God might listen to them and answer when they pray?

- How confident are they about this, do you think?

⊕ investigate

❯ Read Hebrews 10 v 19-22

The writer of this New Testament letter to ethnically Jewish Christians uses imagery from the Old Testament Jewish religion and temple as he describes what Jesus has done for his followers.

2. What can Christians do, and why can we do that (v 19-20)?

• Why is this so remarkable?

3. Explain what the blood of Jesus has done for his people. See Hebrews 9 v 28 and 2 Corinthians 5 v 21.

4. In light of these truths, what should Christians do (Hebrews 10 v 22)?

5. What does it mean to draw near to God with a "sincere heart"? (What is the opposite of a sincere heart?)

A "sincere heart" alone is not enough. In fact, without "the full assurance that faith brings" (v 22), our hearts won't be sincere.

6. What can we be sure of when we have faith in Jesus Christ (see v 22)?

If we are not trusting in Christ to make us righteous, the only alternative is our own righteousness. This is not a recipe for confidence: we will try to hide the messy parts of ourselves from God and other people—our hearts won't be sincere.

⊡ explore more

optional

Paul gives us a great example of confidence in Christ.

❯ Read Philippians 3 v 2-9

Paul warns Christians against false teachers seeking to be righteous by what they do (e.g. by circumcision—a ritual performed on Jewish males as a sign of belonging to God's chosen people; see Genesis 17). Paul argues that true Christians (he calls them "the circumcision", v 3) are those who "boast in" (rely on) Jesus Christ, and don't put any confidence "in the flesh" (in things they or others do).

What were the reasons why Paul was once confident that he was righteous before God?

What kinds of things might we add to our own list?

How does Paul now view these reasons for his past confidence (v 7-8)?

What are the signs that someone is boasting in (relying on) Christ?
Or that someone has gone back to putting confidence in things that
people do?

⊟ apply

7. Why do you think we Christians sometimes don't do what we wonderfully
can do—that is, draw near to God?

8. People around us may have an unfounded confidence that if they pray to
God, he will hear and answer them. What should we be saying to them?

☺ getting personal

If you are confident about praying to God… is that merely because
you are confident of your own righteousness? Make sure your
confidence comes from the power of Jesus' blood to free us from our
sins.

If you struggle to draw near to God in prayer… is that because you
are waiting until you are confident of your own righteousness? You
need to understand that the only reason you can approach the living
God is because of the power of Jesus' blood to free us from our sins.

⊕ investigate

▶ Read Hebrews 4 v 14-16

9. Jesus is the sacrifice for sin, but what other role does he carry out for his people (v 14; see also 10 v 21)?

• See **Hebrews 5 v 1-2 and 7 v 25**: What are the responsibilities of this role (find three)?

• See **Hebrews 7 v 23-27**: How is Jesus far better than the Jewish priests in Jerusalem were (find two things)?

10. Adding to what we have just learned about Jesus our high priest, Hebrews 4 v 14-16 gives us another reason for confidence to approach God. What is that?

➡ apply

11. What light does Hebrews 4 v 14-16 shed on what we should pray for?

• What should we expect to happen as a result?

12. What inadequate views of Jesus do we often have, and how do they affect our confidence to ask for God's help when we are weak and tempted?

⊡ getting personal

Write down some of the temptations that you and your church are facing, for which you can confidently seek God's mercy and grace. Work out how you'll do that in the next week.

⬆ pray

Thank God...

Confess to God...

Ask God...

5 John 15 v 1-17
THROUGH THE SON: PRAYING DEPENDENTLY

The story so far

Our heavenly Father sees and know everything, so we mustn't pray like hypocrites and we needn't pray like pagans.

Jesus teaches that prayer to our heavenly Father is first about seeking his glory and will, and then about asking him to provide for our needs.

Through Jesus, our perfect sacrifice for sins and our sympathetic high priest, we can approach God with confidence that he will meet our needs.

⊕ talkabout

1. If you could ask God for anything, what would you ask for?

⊕ investigate

Last session showed that we should be confident as we pray to God, but our confidence must be based on Jesus Christ—on his sacrifice of atonement on our behalf, and his eternal and pure yet sympathetic priesthood. This session looks at how vital it is to remain completely dependent on Jesus.

▶ Read John 15 v 1-17

In the Old Testament God's people, Israel, were pictured as a vine and were expected to produce fruit for God, but consistently failed (see Hosea 10 v 1). Here, Jesus uses the same vine picture as he teaches his disciples.

2. How does Jesus describe the relationship between himself and his true disciples?

• Why is his picture so helpful?

3. Some branches are dead: some people who look like Jesus' disciples are not. Jesus' words here help us know who are his true disciples. What's the key sign and what does it reveal about a person?

4. How does verse 8 show what it means to bear fruit? And how is that different from simply being a nice or decent person?

5. The word "remain" can also be translated as continue, endure, or stay. What does remaining in Christ involve in practice?
• v 7a: • v 9, then v 10, then v 12-13:

➔ apply

6. What's the warning here if we are not remaining in Christ and producing fruit (v 6), and how should this guide our prayers, do you think?

• What's the uncomfortable truth if we are fruit-bearing branches (v 2), and how should this guide our prayers, do you think?

7. How can we tell that someone (ourselves even) is in danger of "moving on" from Christ instead of remaining in him?

• How can we help each other to remain in Jesus?

⊡ getting personal

Use these questions to check how well you are remaining in Christ:
• When are you most tempted to "move on" from Christ to something that promises to be more exciting or fulfilling?
• How influential are Jesus' words in you?
• How important is it for you to bear fruit that shows you are a disciple of Christ?
Now read **Colossians 2 v 6-9**.

⊡ **explore more**

An incident in Mark's Gospel shows what happens when Jesus' followers forget to depend on him.

▶ **Read Mark 9 v 14-29**

Jesus had recently sent out the Twelve to teach and heal, and with authority over evil spirits (Mark 6 v 7 and 12-13). The disciples have realised that Jesus is the Messiah—the Saviour-King sent from God and promised by him throughout the Old Testament (Mark 8 v 27-30).

How does the failure of the disciples here provide a negative illustration of Jesus' words in John 15?
By contrast, how does the boy's father provide a positive illustration?
How is this at odds with much teaching today about what it means to have faith in God?
How can we make the same mistake as the disciples? And what is the sign that we are making that mistake?

⊡ **investigate** John 15

8. What does Jesus promise in verse 7? To whom?

9. Verse 7 begins, "If you remain in me and my words remain in you…" How then should we understand "ask whatever you wish"? (Compare Psalm 37 v 4.)

10. In light of verse 8, what kinds of things will disciples of Christ wish and ask for, do you think?

11. What does Jesus promise in verse 16? To whom?

 • What does he mean by "ask in my name", do you think? (Look again at verses 9-17.)

⤷ apply

12. Imagine someone tells you, based on Jesus' promises here, that they are asking God for the six-figure salary they want, and they are certain that he will give it to them. What would you say to them?

13. How does this passage guide you:
 • to think more carefully about what you pray for?

 • to be more adventurous about what you pray for?

• to be more thankful in your prayers?

⊡ getting personal

"Ask … and it will be done for you … whatever you ask in my name the Father will give you."
Are you asking God for things? Or are you so worried about "getting it wrong" that you never ask him for anything? Of course we need to be careful to understand Jesus' promises correctly. But then we need to start asking—it's what Jesus wants us to do. What can you ask God for right now?

⬆ pray

Talk to God about the things you have learned this session:

• your need to continue in Christ

• the privilege of your relationship with Christ, the true vine

• the privilege of your purpose in Christ—bearing fruit that will last

6

Romans 8 v 9-30

BY THE SPIRIT:
PRAYING IN WEAKNESS

The story so far

Jesus teaches that prayer to our heavenly Father is first about seeking his glory and will, and then about asking him to provide for our needs.

Through Jesus, our perfect sacrifice for sins and our sympathetic high priest, we can approach God with confidence that he will meet our needs.

When we remain in Jesus, our wishes reflect his concerns and purposes, and he has promised that we will be given whatever we ask for in prayer.

⊕ talkabout

1. What are the main reasons why people don't pray, or give up praying, do you think?

⊥ investigate

❯ Read Romans 8 v 9-17

In this famous passage Paul speaks to those who have become followers of Jesus, and he sets out the privileges and blessings of life "in Christ".

> ### DICTIONARY
>
> **The realm of the flesh (v 9):** under the control of the sinful nature.
> **Abba (v 15):** something like "Daddy" in the Aramaic language.
> **Testifies (v 16):** speaks as a witness.

2. In what way are followers of Jesus different from everyone else (v 9)?

3. In what way are followers of Jesus no different from anyone else (v 10)?

• What does this mean for our expectations about our life in this world?

There is no direct advantage for our physical bodies in becoming a Christian. We continue to be susceptible to illness, injury and ageing, and we are heading for the grave, just like non-Christians.

4. How might this tempt us to live (v 12-13)?

• What will stop us from living like this?

5. Although a Christian's body is still subject to death, the Spirit does change our experience of life in this world. In what ways (v 14-16)?

• How does the Spirit change our perspective on life in this world
(v 11, 17)?

⤷ apply

6. All Christians have the Spirit (v 9). How does that make Christian prayer
different from any other kind? (Review what we've learned about the
Spirit's work in us and think about how that affects our praying.)

7. This passage shows what Jesus' followers can and can't expect in this life.
How does this guide our praying, for ourselves or others:
• in sickness?

• when facing death?

• when struggling to overcome a particular sin?

• when feeling far from God?

• when suffering for following Jesus?

⊡ getting personal

Are there ways in which, as a Christian, you expect too much in this
life, because you forget that you haven't yet been resurrected? Or do
you expect too little, because you haven't understood the difference
it makes to be led by the Spirit? How do you need to change your
expectations? How will this change your prayers?

⬇ investigate

▶ Read Romans 8 v 18-30

8. In what way do verses 18-21 reflect what we have already learned in verses 9-11?

• What does this mean for our expectations about this world?

So far in Romans 8, we have seen that our bodies are dying and we live in a world marked by frustration and decay. We struggle with temptations to sin; we groan along with the rest of creation; we are not "at home" in this life; we suffer; we are weak.

9. How does our weakness show itself (v 26)?

• How does the Spirit help us (v 26-27)?

10. In outline, what will the Spirit ask God for on our behalf (v 27-30)?

➔ apply

11. Think of situations in which Christians don't know what to pray for (perhaps one you face right now). In each situation:
• even so, what should you still do?

• what can you be confident about?

• what do you now know you can pray for?

• How will the promise that the Spirit helps us in our weakness comfort us in times of distress?

⊡ getting personal

Weak yet confident. Dying yet alive. Groaning yet filled with hope.
This is what it means to live in this world as a follower of Jesus, with
the Spirit of God living in us.
How much do you thank God for his gift to you of the Holy Spirit?
How will you seek the help of the Holy Spirit in everyday life?

⊡ explore more

optional

Another source of weakness in God's people comes from God's
enemy, the devil, scheming against us and trying to destroy our faith
in Christ.

▶ Read Ephesians 6 v 10-20

*How could you summarise the armour of God in one or two words?
Prayer is part of defending ourselves against the devil (v 18). Who are
we to pray for, when and how?
What does "pray in the Spirit" (v 18) mean, do you think? (See v 17.)
Look at Paul's situation when he wrote this letter (v 20; see also 3 v 1
and 4 v 1). What would most of us want others to pray for us in this
situation?
How is Paul's prayer request for himself (v 19-20) shaped by his
understanding of how Christians resist the devil?*

⊡ pray

"The Spirit of God lives in you."
Read through the passage again, taking note of all the wonderful
firstfruits of the Spirit that Christians have. Then spend time thanking and
praising God for his goodness to you.

7 1 Corinthians 14 v 1–25
BY THE SPIRIT: PRAYING TO SERVE

The story so far

Through Jesus, our perfect sacrifice for sins and our sympathetic high priest, we can approach God with confidence that he will meet our needs.

When we remain in Jesus, our wishes reflect his concerns and purposes, and he has promised that we will be given whatever we ask for in prayer.

In this world we will be weak, yet we can be confident because the Spirit helps us in many ways and intercedes for us when we don't know what to pray.

⊕ talkabout

1. How important do you think it is for Christians to pray publicly when they meet together? Why do you think that?

⊕ investigate

In 1 Corinthians 14, Paul is in the middle of teaching about the Spirit's work and gifts in the church. In that context he gives instructions about what Christians should and should not do when meeting together. Let's first look at what Paul has said just previously.

2. **Read 1 Corinthians 12 v 4-11.** What is the purpose of the gifts of the Spirit?

3. **Read 1 Corinthians 12 v 27-31.** What else do we learn about the Spirit's gifts?

4. Paul tells the Corinthians, "Eagerly desire the greater gifts" (v 31). What does he mean by "greater gifts", do you think? (See also 14 v 1.)

▶ Read 1 Corinthians 14 v 1-17 and 22-25

Paul compares two gifts of the Spirit: prophecy, which, his contrast shows, is a greater gift; and speaking in a tongue, clearly portrayed here as a lesser gift.

5. What exactly is Paul talking about when he refers to speaking in a tongue (see v 2 and 13-15)?

DICTIONARY

Prophecy / prophesy (v 1, 3): speaking truth from God.
Tongue (v 2): another language (maybe not a known human one; see 13 v 1).
Edifies (v 4): encourages moral/spiritual improvement.
Sign (v 22): something that points you to a destination—here, unbelief or belief.
Convicted (v 24): brought to an understanding of the truth, which reveals your guilt.

6. What does prophesying achieve that speaking/praying in a tongue fails to achieve (v 4; see also v 23-25)?

• Fill in the table below to contrast the effects of prophesying with those of speaking/praying in a tongue.

EFFECTS OF PROPHESYING	EFFECTS OF SPEAKING IN A TONGUE
v 3	v 2
v 4	v 4
v 16 (What should happen here?)	v 11
v 19	v 16
v 24-25	v 23

• Why do you think Paul says that for a church to desire the greater gifts (like prophecy) is to "follow the way of love" (v 1)?

7. What important purpose does praying in a tongue achieve (v 2)?

> • Why is this not a good enough reason for Paul to commend praying in a tongue when Christians meet together?

8. What insight does Paul's reasoning give us into the purpose of praying publicly?

⊡ apply

Think about praying in public (anything from a prayer partnership or small Bible-study group to a church prayer meeting or service).

9. How will your praying be affected by knowing that you are not only speaking to God but to edify fellow believers and witness to unbelievers?

10. In what ways might our prayers be unintelligible to those around us?

⊡ getting personal

Paul's passion when he meets with other Christians is not to give free expression to his spirit, but to use his Spirit-filled mind so that others are instructed, edified and convicted by the Spirit-revealed truth from God.

If you pray publicly, think how you may need to change your praying, so that through you the Spirit can edify others even more.
If you've never prayed publicly, ask God for the Spirit's help to build up someone else as you pray aloud with them.

⊡ explore more

optional

> **Read Acts 4 v 23-31**

Here's a clear example of the New Testament church praying publicly together—Christians "rais[ing] their voices together in prayer to God".

What situation propelled the Christians to pray (see v 1-4, 18-22)?
What was the theme of their praying (v 24-28)?
What informed their praying?
  • v 25-26   *• v 27-28*
What's surprising about their request? (How might we have prayed differently?)

Think about how this illustrates what we have learned this session:
How did these Christians use their minds as they prayed (compare 1 Corinthians 14 v 14-15)?
How can we see that people were edified by this prayer?

⊡ apply

11. How do our prayers sound when we pray with a mind informed by the gospel and enlightened by the Spirit? What things might we start praying for, or stop praying for?

⊡ getting personal

At the end of this series of Bible studies, write down some of the things you personally have learned or re-learned about real prayer—praying to the Father, through the Son, by the Spirit.

⊡ pray

On your own... ask God to help you by his Spirit to pray in a way that edifies fellow believers and witnesses to unbelievers.

Together... put into practice what you've learned this session as you pray together, praising God for all that you have learned about the privilege of prayer, and trusting the Spirit to use your prayers to build up Christ's people.

Real prayer

LEADER'S GUIDE

Real prayer: Leader's Guide

INTRODUCTION

Leading a Bible study can be a bit like herding cats—everyone has a different idea of what the passage could be about, and a different line of enquiry that they want to pursue. But a good group leader is more than someone who just referees this kind of discussion. You will want to:

- correctly understand and handle the Bible passage. But also...

- encourage and train the people in your group to do this for themselves. Don't fall into the trap of spoon-feeding people by simply passing on the information in the Leader's Guide. Then...

- make sure that no Bible study is finished without everyone knowing how the passage is relevant for them. What changes do you all need to make in the light of the things you have been learning? And finally...

- encourage the group to turn all that has been learned and discussed into prayer.

Your Bible-study group is unique, and you are likely to know better than anyone the capabilities, backgrounds and circumstances of the people you are leading. That's why we've designed these guides with a number of optional features. If they're a quiet bunch, you might want to spend longer on talkabout. If your time is limited, you can choose to skip explore more, or get people to look at these questions at home. Can't get enough of Bible study? Well, some studies have optional extra homework projects. As leader, you can adapt and select the material to the needs of your particular group.

So what's in the Leader's Guide? The main thing that this Leader's Guide will help you to do is to understand the major teaching points in the passage you are studying, and how to apply them. As well as guidance on the questions, the Leader's Guide for each session contains the following important sections:

THE BIG IDEA

One key sentence will give you the main point of the session. This is what you should be aiming to have fixed in people's minds as they leave the Bible study. And it's the point you need to head back towards when the discussion goes off at a tangent.

SUMMARY

An overview of the passage, including plenty of useful historical background information.

OPTIONAL EXTRA

Usually this is an introductory activity that ties in with the main theme of the Bible study, and is designed to "break the ice" at the beginning of a session. Or it may be a "homework project" that people can tackle during the week.

So let's take a look at the various different features of a Good Book Guide:

⊕ talkabout

Each session kicks off with a discussion question, based on the group's opinions or experiences. It's designed to get people talking and thinking in a general way about the main subject of the Bible study.

⬇ investigate

The first thing you and your group need to know is what the Bible passage is about, which is the purpose of these questions. But watch out—people may come up with answers based on their experiences or teaching they have heard in the past, without referring to the passage at all. It's amazing how often we can get through a Bible study without actually looking at the Bible! If you're stuck for an answer, the Leader's Guide contains guidance for questions. These are the answers to direct your group to. This information isn't meant to be read out to people—ideally, you want them to discover these answers from the Bible for themselves. Sometimes there are optional follow-up questions (see ☑ in guidance on questions) to help you help your group get to the answer.

⊡ explore more

These questions generally point people to other relevant parts of the Bible. They are useful for helping your group to see how the passage fits into the "big picture" of the whole Bible. These sections are OPTIONAL—only use them if you have time. Remember that it's better to finish in good time having really grasped one big thing from the passage, than to try and cram everything in.

⮕ apply

We want to encourage you to spend more time working at application—too often, it is simply tacked on at the end. In the Good Book Guides, apply sections are mixed in with the investigate sections of the study. We hope that people will realise that application is not just an optional extra, but rather, the whole purpose of studying the

Bible. We do Bible study so that our lives can be changed by what we hear from God's word. If you skip the application, the Bible study hasn't achieved its purpose.

These questions draw out practical lessons that we can all learn from the Bible passage. You can review what has been learned so far, and think about practical differences that this should make in our churches and our lives. The group gets the opportunity to talk about what they personally have learned.

☺ getting personal

These can be done at home, but it is well worth allowing a few moments of quiet reflection during the study for each person to think and pray about specific changes they need to make in their own lives. Why not have a time for reporting back at the beginning of the following session, so that everyone can be encouraged and challenged by one another to make application a priority?

⬆ pray

In Acts 4 v 25-30 the first Christians quoted Psalm 2 as they prayed in response to the persecution of the apostles by the Jewish religious leaders. Today however, it's not as common for Christians to base prayers on the truths of God's word as it once was. As a result, our prayers tend to be weak, superficial and self-centred rather than bold, visionary and God-centred.

The prayer section is based on what has been learned from the Bible passage. How different our prayer times would be if we were genuinely responding to what God has said to us through his word.

1 Luke 18 v 9-14
WHY PRAY?

THE BIG IDEA
Real prayer starts with sinners humbly asking God for mercy; and God answers by justifiying them in Jesus Christ.

SUMMARY
The Bible says a lot about prayer, but—surprisingly perhaps—it doesn't specifically answer the question: why pray? The Bible assumes that it's important and right to pray to God. But it also raises a problem: "Your iniquities have separated you from your God; your sins have hidden his face from you, so that he will not hear" (Isaiah 59 v 2).

This should be a worrying indication that our prayers might not be real—that although we think we are talking to God, we fail to "connect" with him because he chooses not to listen to sinful rebels. So does God listen to any prayers, and if so, what kind of prayers does he answer?

Jesus' story of two men in the temple, contrasting a prayer that God won't listen to with a prayer that he wonderfully answers, reveals the first and foundational reason for why we should pray, and the kind of prayer that will connect us with the One who will be our heavenly Father.

Real prayer means we throw ourselves on God's mercy. It involves humbling ourselves: admitting our sinfulness and that we deserve nothing from God. But Jesus also wants us to see that God is merciful; real prayer means trusting him. He loves to show mercy to sinners, and he will do that because of Jesus' death on the cross. There are further reasons to pray (see question 10): all involve the same humility combined with trust in

God's mercy that the tax collector showed.

OPTIONAL EXTRA
If the group know each other, get people to show how good they are at something (making a cake; parallel-parking) by comparing themselves with someone who does it terribly. (This is how the Pharisee tries to justify himself before God.) Others could show the opposite by comparing them with someone much better. Or, show the famous class sketch from the 1960s' UK TV show The Frost Report (a clip is available on YouTube). (Links with Q4 and 5.)

GUIDANCE FOR QUESTIONS
1. How do you answer the question: why pray? There are many possible answers but we are about to see the foundational reason: because we are sinners and need God's mercy. All real prayer starts here, as Jesus' story of the Pharisee and the tax collector shows.

2. … What do the following passages reveal about Pharisees, tax collectors, and Jesus? (See table at top of next page.)

3. Contrast the two men in Jesus' parable. (See second table on next page.)

• **The Pharisee isn't lying when he says: "I am not like … this tax collector", so what's the problem with saying this?** The Pharisee lists sins that he hasn't committed, but Jesus has pointed out that outwardly respectable, religious people like the Pharisees are guilty of sins of the heart e.g. idolatry (16 v 13-15), and judging others (18 v 9). These are less

	PHARISEES	TAX COLLECTORS	JESUS
Luke 15 v 1-7	Criticised Jesus for eating with "sinners" (v 2)	Gathered round to hear Jesus (v 1)	Ate with tax collectors; told a parable showing heaven's joy over a repentant sinner (v 3-7)
Luke 16 v 13-15	Loved money; sneered at Jesus (v 14)		Told the Pharisees some hard truths: they can't serve both God and money (v 13); and though they think they are justified, God finds their hearts destestable (v 15)

THINK ABOUT...	THE PHARISEE	THE TAX COLLECTOR
their way of life	Follows religious rules, like fasting and tithing (v 12), and is pleased with himself for doing this	Only knows that he is a sinner (v 13)
their posture in the temple	"Stood by himself" (v 11); he separated himself from others	"Stood at a distance" (perhaps away from the Pharisee), not looking up to heaven, and beating his breast (showing distress) (v 13)
what they pray about or for	Thanks God that he is not like other people (v 11), and lists his religious works (v 12)	Simply asks God for mercy (v 13)

visible to people but detestable to God. And Pharisees reject Jesus, the one sent by God (15 v 2; 16 v 14). The Pharisee's problem is self-righteousness—believing that he is righteous because of his religious observance when in fact he is deeply unrighteous.

4. ... What is the real focus of [the Pharisee's] prayer? Himself—notice how many times he says "I".

• **What, then, would you say is the real purpose of his prayer?** Under the guise of thanking God, he compares himself with others (but only bad'uns) to show how religiously upright, and therefore righteous, he is. This is not a real prayer.

5. Compare the tax collector's prayer. How is it opposite to the Pharisee's prayer? The Pharisee speaks about himself; the tax collector cries to God. The Pharisee parades his good deeds; the tax collector confesses that he is a sinner. The Pharisee compares himself favourably with "sinners"; the tax collector looks only to God. The Pharisee is confident; the tax collector humbly throws himself on God's mercy.

• **How does Jesus show that this kind of prayer "works"?** Jesus says the tax collector "went home justified before God" (v 14). God showed him mercy by declaring him not guilty.

6. Why does Jesus tell this story (v 9)? For the benefit of those who were "confident of their own righteousness and looked down on everyone else".

• **What is his message to these people (and us)?** If we are confident of our own righteousness, like the Pharisee, we exalt ourselves; and God will humble us (v 14). We need to humble ourselves, like the tax collector, confessing that we are sinners and crying out to God for mercy. If we do this, God will show mercy: he will exalt and justify us.

7. From this story, especially verse 14, how do you think Jesus would answer the question: Why pray? Everyone— whether guilty or self-righteous—needs to pray like the tax collector. We are all sinners, all needing to be justified; we all need to ask God for mercy. Nothing we can do, however religiously correct or superior to others, will result in a "not guilty" verdict from God. The first and foundational reason for praying is our need of God's mercy to justify us.

• **How would he answer the question: What kind of prayer moves God to act?** It's prayer in which we humble ourselves—confessing that we are sinners, refraining from parading before God any of our good or religious acts, asking God

to show mercy, and acknowledging that we have no right to demand, and don't deserve, anything good from God.

8. APPLY: What antidote to [Pharisee-type prayers] have we seen (see question 2, 15 v 1), and how can we encourage this antidote in our own lives and churches? The tax collectors came to hear Jesus' teaching (15 v 1), whereas the Pharisees looked for reasons not to listen to him (v 2; 16 v 14). It's God's word that reveals God's character, our sinfulness, and Jesus' sacrificial death for sinners. Only understanding our sinfulness will lead us to pray like the tax collector. Left to ourselves, we wrongly think we are all right—imperfect, yes, but basically good. God's word, however, demolishes this view of ourselves. When people and churches neglect teaching and living out God's word, there is growing Pharisaism: self-righteousness, outward religion, lack of compassion towards "sinners", and finally hostility to the gospel. Discuss ways—in your lives, relationships and church activities— that you could share, for example, how God's word has enlightened, convicted or encouraged you; or how you could confess sin to one another.

9. APPLY: What antidote to [prayer-inhibiting shame and guilt] have we seen (see question 2, 15 v 3-7), and how can we encourage this antidote in our own lives and churches? The tax collector could not have prayed his prayer if he didn't understand that God shows mercy. (Remember how Jesus had told a crowd that included tax collectors his parable of the lost sheep in 15 v 3-7.) We need to understand that God loves to show mercy to sinners, and he will do that because of Jesus' death on the cross. Discuss what encourages you to trust in God's mercy and how that can be passed on to others.

**EXPLORE MORE [Acts 17 v 24-31]
What reasons for why we should pray can you work out from what Paul says here? (See v 25, 27, 30 and 31.)** We need God (v 25). God wants us to seek him, and he is not far from us (v 27). God commands us to repent, and warns us of the day when he will judge the world with justice (v 30-31); if we do not repent, we will suffer the punishment of God's just judgment.
What here should humble us? God doesn't need us; we need him. God commands us to repent, and will judge us.
… and what should encourage us to pray? God wants us to seek him; and he isn't far from any of one of us. He's far more wonderful than our wrong views of him.
Imagine someone asks you to explain prayer. Use this passage to explain why humbly asking God for mercy is the only way to truly pray. Practise retelling what Paul says in this passage in your own words.

10. Followers of Jesus have now received God's mercy in Christ. So why do we need to keep praying? Emphasise that other reasons to pray (like those listed below) follow the first and foundational reason—praying for God's mercy to justify us. Only prayer based on this foundation is real prayer that connects us with God (see Isaiah 59 v 2). **Find reasons from the following passages:**
• **Luke 21 v 34-36:** Christians can be tempted away from living for Jesus by pleasures or worries. If we don't resist these temptations, the danger is that on the day of judgment we will not be counted among Christ's people. Jesus warns his followers to watch and pray so that we will persevere as Christ's people

(Matthew 26 v 41; Hebrews 10 v 36-39).
• **Rom. 15 v 30-32:** Paul asks for prayer for very practical things: to be kept safe from enemies of the gospel and for a favourable reception in Jerusalem. By praying like this for other Christians, we participate in their struggle and work for God.
• **1 Timothy 2 v 1-4:** Paul urges Christians to pray for rulers and governments, and for peace in our communities because God "wants all people to be saved and to come to a knowledge of the truth" (v 4). We pray like this not to gain comfortable lives, but to aid the preaching of the gospel.
• **How do these reasons to keep praying underline the lessons of Jesus' parable in Luke 18?** Jesus taught that we need God's mercy, and will receive it when we seek it humbly. Temptations, enemies of the gospel, and rulers are all powerful and beyond our control. So we need God's help. We don't deserve it and have no right to it; yet, because God is merciful, we can pray to him about all these things with humble confidence.

11. APPLY: Write down the last three things you have prayed for. If your prayers rarely reflect the themes of Christian prayer highlighted in Q10, why do you think that might be? Ask people to share what they have written. It may be that we don't really think we need God's help; like the Pharisee, we have too "exalted" a view of ourselves. Or perhaps we don't see God as merciful; we may think that God can't be interested in us (not true), or that since we don't deserve his help (true), there's no point in trying to speak to him (not true). Even the shame-filled tax collector didn't draw this conclusion. We can come to God—and can only come—in both humility and trust.

2 Matthew 6 v 5-8
TO THE FATHER:
HOW NOT TO PRAY

THE BIG IDEA

Because of who we pray to—our heavenly Father, who sees and knows everything—we mustn't pray like hypocrites and we needn't pray like pagans.

SUMMARY

We've seen Jesus teach that those who humble themselves will receive mercy from God (be justified)—something we all need because our sins have separated us from God, so that he will not hear us.

In the Sermon on the Mount Jesus teaches his disciples—those justified by God—rather than the crowd around them. He makes a claim unique to Christianity: that God is their heavenly Father. This truth profoundly affects how Christians pray. In this first look at teaching from the Sermon on the Mount, Jesus shows how real prayer is different from the praying of hypocrites and of pagans.

We see that hypocrites pray to impress other people; they don't speak to God. They "pray" looking to their reputation with other people, rather than God's mercy in Christ, to make themselves feel acceptable to God. Meanwhile pagans use words to manipulate, or pester, or apply a formula to get what

they want from a "divine vending machine"; they don't really talk, and it's not to the real God. They look to techniques and rituals to get what they want in life.

Here we are challenged to grow in the relationship with God already established by Jesus, by speaking to our heavenly Father about our needs, trusting that he is both able and willing to provide.

OPTIONAL EXTRA

Divide the group into two to play charades. Explain the rules (see Wikipedia). Each team chooses an actor. Give the word "hypocrite" to one actor and "pagan" to the other, with definitions from "Dictionary" (Study Guide, p14) if needed. Time how long it takes each team to discover their mystery word. In this study we see Jesus teaching us not to pray like hypocrites (Qs 4-6) or pagans (Qs 8-9).

GUIDANCE FOR QUESTIONS

1. List some of the privileges and joys of a good father/child relationship. You could compare this relationship with that of a boss and employee. See the table below for some suggestions.

FATHER/CHILD	BOSS/EMPLOYEE
Bound together by love	Bound together by a contract
Part of the family for ever	Part of company till resignation/dismissal
Can call upon each other at any time for any reason	Can only call upon each other to fulfil contractual duties
Child inherits share of family property	Employee only paid (no share in company)

2. Read Matthew 5 v 1-2. Who is Jesus particularly speaking to in the Sermon on the Mount? Although crowds are there, it is the disciples who come to Jesus, and they whom Jesus begins to teach.

• **Why is it important to be clear about this, do you think?** It shows that the Sermon on the Mount is teaching for Jesus' followers. It describes those who belong to him, and not how to become his follower.

3. How does Jesus choose to describe God's relationship with Jesus' followers in these verses? If God is our Father in heaven, then we are his children.

• **This view of God is unique to the Bible. What does it say about God?** He has created us to live in a close, warm relationship with him. He loves us, unlike the gods of other religions, who only rule or manipulate. **And what does it say about us?** In right relationship with God, we become part of his family, with all the protection, provision and privileges which that entails. God's fatherhood also denotes his loving authority over us, and our dependence on him.
(**Note:** If some have experienced a painful or abusive relationship with their human father, emphasise that God is the perfect Father—he is what we would wish all earthly fathers to be like.)

4. How do hypocrites pray (v 5)? Where they can be seen and heard by others. Jesus calls them hypocrites because although they look as though they are speaking to God, actually they are not—they are merely acting to look religious. Their prayers are not real.

• **Why do they pray like that?** To impress the people who see them and earn a reputation for being religiously devout.

5. What is Jesus' antidote here to hypocritical prayer (v 6)? To pray where no one else can see us; then we will be truly talking to God, rather than performing to other people.

6. What truth about God does Jesus highlight to expose the hypocrites' wrong thinking (v 6)? God sees what is done in secret: both behind the closed door of our room, and in our hearts (as we pray in public). The hypocrites seem to think that God can be deceived, like other people, by their outward behaviour; or that it doesn't matter what God sees. Jesus completely refutes their view of God.

• **How will this encourage us to pray to God privately?** Praying to God in private is never a waste of time, because he sees and rewards us. But praying to impress others is certainly a waste of time; the only benefit is that others see us—yet they can't give us anything we need.

⊠

• **What is the reward in verse 6, do you think?** Most likely, it's that God answers our prayer by giving us what we need (see also verse 8—the parallel sentence in the next section, on pagan prayer).

7. APPLY: … When we don't pray privately, how does it reveal our wrong view… • of God? We don't look to him for what we need, especially for justification (to be made good and acceptable to God). Instead, we seek this from how others view us, believing we are good because people see us as religiously devout. So we view God as easily deceived or manipulated, and not perfectly upholding truth, righteousness and justice; we haven't understood why Jesus needed to die for sins. Or, from fear of

God's verdict on us, we turn to impressing other people to feel good enough about ourselves. So we view God as without grace; we haven't understood the significance of what Jesus achieved on the cross. **• of the purpose and value of prayer?** Prayer shows our apparent goodness to other people, but in itself has no value. It's only a religious hoop to jump through; it's not intimate conversation with our heavenly Father.

• When we pray like the hypocrites, what are we depending on to feel good about ourselves and to impress God? On a ritual or good deed ticked off. If we do enough of these to make people think we're very good, perhaps God will think that too. We are not depending on Jesus and the relationship we can have with God through him—as the loved, though needy, children of our perfect Father, who will give us everything we need.

8. How do pagans pray (Matt 6 v 7)? They "keep on babbling". Other translations mention "empty phrases" (ESV) and "meaningless repetition" (NASB). Instead of communicating substance, pagans focus on length or repetition of prayers. They are not talking to God; they don't connect with him.

• Why do they pray like that? They think that the more words they say, the more likely it is that God will hear them. They think God is distant, and either uncaring or unable to hear; and prayer is viewed as something like pester power, or coins put into a vending machine. (1 Kings 18 v 26-29 gives a real-life example of pagan prayer.)

9. What truth about God does Jesus highlight that will encourage his followers to pray differently from the pagans (v 8)? Our perfect heavenly Father knows what we need before we ask him.

• How does Jesus want us to pray, do you think, based on understanding this truth about God? Simply and honestly—acknowledging our needs and asking for our Father's help; and confidently—knowing that he perfectly loves his children, and that he is not far away, deaf, preoccupied or uninterested.

10. If our Father knows all our needs before we even ask him (v 8), what is the purpose of praying to him about these things, do you think? (Look at Paul's experience in 2 Corinthians 1 v 8-11.) Prayer isn't for God's benefit (except that he delights in providing for his children)—he knows precisely what we need without us speaking to him. It's for our benefit—so that we grow in the children-and-Father relationship already established by Jesus between his followers and God. By praying, we acknowledge our need and our dependence on him, and learn to trust that he is our perfect Father in heaven, able and willing to provide everything we need, as we see him answer our prayers. In Asia Paul and his companions despaired of life itself and so had to rely on God, "who raises the dead" (v 8-9). Paul shares how God answered their prayer for deliverance to encourage other Christians to pray for him (v 10-11), so that they in turn would grow in their trust of and thanksgiving to God as they continued to see him answer prayer.

EXPLORE MORE [Luke 11 v 5-13]
Why did the man in the parable get the bread that he needed (v 8)? He believed his friend would help if he asked him; that's why, although the friend was reluctant at first, the man kept asking until he was given

the bread.

What's the difference between the friend (v 7-8) and our Father God? God won't tell us not to bother him. Point out that Jesus is not contradicting Matthew 6 v 7. We needn't approach God in the way that this man approached his friend because God isn't like the friend. But even with such a dismal friend, the man knew it was worth asking him for what he needed. How much more worthwhile is it to ask God for help!

Since God our Father is not like our human friends, what does Jesus say we should do, and what can we be confident of (v 9-10)? We should come to God and request his help with the things we need (asking, seeking and knocking are all different descriptions of doing this); and be confident that he will answer and give us what we need.

How does Jesus show that it is illogical and unreasonable to doubt that God can and will answer our prayers (v 11-13)? Even earthly fathers, who are all sinful, give good things when their children ask. How then can we doubt that our perfect Father in heaven will give us all we need?

11. APPLY: What pagan-type praying is popular today in your local community and culture? (Think about how people pray and how they talk about prayer.) Answers might include: praying in a special place; following special rituals; looking to "experts" to pray for them; "boosting" prayer with things like fasting; using special words; bargaining with God. Many think of prayer as "positive thinking" or psychic energy. Many only "pray" in emergencies. These are all attempts to manipulate or impress. They are not real prayer: talking to the real, living God in the way which we can be confident that he will hear and answer.

- **Why might we sometimes find these ways of praying attractive?** They appeal to our pride—we can contribute to the outcome partially through our own efforts and "goodness". Also we can bypass a relationship with God, approaching him instead as a "divine vending machine". We don't have to think about the state of our hearts or how we live outside the "religious part" of our lives.

- **How does this study help you want to pray in a Christian way, and not in a pagan way?** As we've seen, God is unimaginably greater and better than a "divine vending machine". He is our Creator, Provider and Judge—we need him and we're accountable to him. And through Jesus Christ we can come to know him as our heavenly Father—we can speak to him, trust him and enjoy his presence and care.

12. APPLY: Jesus' antidote for pagan-type praying is trust in God's perfect provision for all our needs. How can we help each other grow in this trust? Perhaps by reminding ourselves of God's faithful past provision—both from Scripture and in our own lives (keeping a record of answered prayers is helpful); by sharing God's faithfulness with others—through testimonies or prayers of thanksgiving; by our example of trusting him for present and future needs. Helpful settings for these things include prayer partnerships and one-to-one mentoring, hospitality, deeper and more personal conversations than our normal chit-chat, prayer meetings, and using all the modes of communication and social media at our disposal more intentionally for the purpose of building up each other.

3 Matthew 6 v 9-15
TO THE FATHER: HOW TO PRAY

THE BIG IDEA
Jesus teaches that Christian prayer to our heavenly Father is first about seeking his glory and will, and then about asking him to provide for our needs.

SUMMARY
We've seen Jesus tell us not to pray like hypocrites or pagans because God is our perfect Father in heaven. But how should we pray? This session looks phrase by phrase at Jesus' answer to that question: the Lord's Prayer.

We shouldn't be surprised that all the teaching of the Bible leads us to the cross of Christ, and that's certainly true of the Lord's Prayer. As we look at the first three God-centred requests in light of what the Bible teaches elsewhere, we see that each one is about the gospel.

God's name is hallowed by the message that Jesus is the fulfilment of his promise of an eternal King, and the Redeemer of his people, through his sacrificial death on the cross. God's kingdom comes as people respond with faith to the message about Jesus, and share it with others. God's will is done as his people, redeemed by Jesus, live transformed lives distinctive from those around them.

The second three requests detail what we most need: our daily bread, forgiveness and deliverance from the evil one. Again, our need of Jesus and his gospel are central. But our prayers often don't reflect these themes of the Lord's Prayer. We're challenged to start praying about God's concerns and our true needs—things we can be confident God will give.

OPTIONAL EXTRA
Memorise the Lord's Prayer (Matthew 6 v 9-13) in ten minutes or less. (1) Write it on a whiteboard. Read it through a few times together. Use dice to decide how many words can be removed between each reading. (2) Divide the Lord's Prayer into phrases written onto cards. Beginning at the end of the prayer, wrap them into layers of a parcel; the first to be unwrapped will be the beginning of the prayer. Pass the parcel; each person who unwraps a layer has to recite from the beginning of the prayer before reading their card.

GUIDANCE FOR QUESTIONS
Note: This study covering the whole of the Lord's Prayer is fairly long. You could break it into two after the Getting Personal section that follows question 6.

1. What would you say about the Lord's Prayer to someone who doesn't know anything about it? Answers will indicate how well people know the Lord's Prayer and what attitudes towards it they may have grown up with.

"Our Father in heaven"
2. How does this way of addressing God show: • that we can be confident when we pray? God is our Father. A good father welcomes his children, however they

feel and whatever they've done. We can be confident that our perfect Father won't reject us when we pray to him. • **that we need to be humble when we pray?** Our Father in heaven is sovereign over the universe and perfect in his justice and holiness. He doesn't need us or anything we can give or do; but we need him for absolutely everything.

"Hallowed be your name"

3. Read part of David's prayer in 2 Samuel 7 v 22-26. What two things done by God for his people make his name great? (1) He redeemed his people through great and awesome wonders (v 23). (2) He has made a promise to David and his family—to put a son of David on the throne for ever—and he will keep his promise (v 25-26). God's name is hallowed by the redemption of his people and the reign of the one he has chosen to be King of his kingdom.

- **Read John 12 v 23-24, 27-28. What is Jesus speaking about that will make God's name great?** His imminent death; God's name will be glorified through Jesus' death (v 28).

- **In light of these passages, what should we pray for when we ask God to hallow his name?** God's name is most glorified by the gospel—the message that, through his death on the cross, Jesus would redeem God's people and become the everlasting King of God's kingdom. So praying "Hallowed be your name" means praying that the gospel will be preached and heard, and people brought into God's kingdom.

"Your kingdom come"

4. [Look at the following NT truths.] Now work out what it means in practice

to pray, **"Your kingdom come".** Perhaps three sub-groups could discuss one point each.

- **The kingdom of God comes when the gospel is preached (Luke 10 v 1, 9-11, 16); we see it when we see who Jesus is (9 v 27-29); and we enter it by becoming a follower of Jesus (18 v 18-25).** We need to pray for people to see the truth about Jesus, and to be persuaded to give up whatever is necessary to follow him.

- **The kingdom of God is seen when Jesus' followers live in a way that pleases God (see Romans 14 v 17-18).** We need to pray that Christ's followers will be filled with the Spirit and live lives of godliness—rather than legalism and hypocrisy—which will be a witness to people around us.

- **The kingdom of God will come fully at the end of history when Jesus returns (Luke 21 v 27-31).** We need to pray for Christ's triumphant return, which will usher in the new creation (see also Revelation 22 v 17, 20). By and large, this isn't a prayer we hear in our churches.

"Your will be done, on earth as it is in heaven"

5. ... What ,then, [from the following passages] should Christians be praying for when we ask, "Your will be done"? Again, three sub-groups could discuss one passage each.

- **1 Thessalonians 4 v 3:** For help to live a holy life, particularly in regard to our sexuality and how we use our bodies.

- **1 Thessalonians 5 v 16-18:** For help to cultivate joy, thankfulness and prayerful dependence on him.

- **1 Peter 2 v 13-15:** For help to submit to human authorities and not to be subversive or rebellious.

Note that all these passages show God's will is done as Christians live godly lives.

- **How do you think Christians living out God's will in these areas compare with those around them?** Identify the opposites of God's will outlined here; discuss how widespread these things are in our culture and the effect on those around us when we live God's way in these areas.

6. APPLY: Look again at what we've learned in questions 3 to 5. What can we do that will most hallow God's name, promote God's kingdom and do God's will in this world? For ourselves, persevere in faith in Christ, shown in the gospel we preach and the lives we live. For others, share with them the message about Jesus and pray that they would trust in him.

- **Write down some things you have been challenged to start praying about.** Give people a few moments to note down their answers. You could ask them to share what they have written, or suggest revisiting this in the following session to see if it has made any difference to what you all pray for.

Note: *The best place to divide this study into two is after the Getting Personal section following Q6 in the Study Guide.*

"Give us today our daily bread"
7. Why the focus on "today", do you think? Jesus teaches us to ask God each day for the "bread" we need. Because of our constant tendency to self-sufficiency, trusting in the stuff we amass and ignoring God (see Proverbs 30 v 8-9; Luke 12 v 13-21), there's never a day when we don't need to make this request. It returns us to right and continual dependence on God. This isn't something we can get sorted once

for all and then move on. **And why only "bread"?** Bread was, and still is, the staple food for most people. It symbolises all we need, rather than all we want. (See also Matthew 6 v 8, 25-34.)

- **What can make it difficult for us to ask like this from our heavenly Father?** Forgetting God's daily gracious goodness, and our complete dependence on him. Acting as if we're entitled to his good gifts; or as if our bank balances and our ability to earn provide for us instead. Forgetting what we once were, and starting to believe that we ourselves are morally good—meaning that Jesus, the bread of life, becomes irrelevant in our daily lives.

"And forgive us our debts, as we also have forgiven our debtors"
8. Jesus teaches in Matthew 6 that his disciples need to seek God's forgiveness each day. But what must we do first and why? (See also verses 14-15.) "Debts" = "sins"; compare v 12 and v 14-15. Jesus teaches that we can only ask and expect God to forgive our sins daily if we show that same attitude of grace to others. Refusal to forgive someone disqualifies us from receiving God's forgiveness.

- **How do Jesus' words here fit with the Bible's teaching that we are made right with God through his grace (e.g. Ephesians 2 v 8-9), and not through anything we do?** Jesus' words ("as we also have forgiven") are not about salvation (how to enter his kingdom) but discipleship (how a member of his kingdom lives). Christ's people don't just sign up to intellectual beliefs; their lives are transformed by God's grace—so they forgive others as God has forgiven them. (See Ephesians 2 v 10.) Jesus is saying that we cannot kid ourselves that our right words and beliefs mean we've been saved from sin, if we're not also growing a God-like heart.

"And lead us not into temptation, but deliver us from the evil one"
9. What do you think will ensure that a difficult experience leads to maturity in faith, rather than into sin of some kind? There's a clue in the request: "Deliver us from the evil one". God has a good purpose for our lives that governs why he sometimes allows us to go through trials. But the devil will try to use our trials for his own ends—to destroy our faith, and the unity and love of God's people. So this request makes us look to our heavenly Father, asking him to "lead us". And being led by God will involve both trusting him and listening to him—trusting in his good purposes for us as we go through hard times, and trusting that he will use these experiences to mature us in faith; and being determined to listen to God's word continually and act on it. It may be helpful to think about Adam and Eve in Genesis 3 v 1-6. Why did they do what the devil wanted? What should they have done to escape his trap? A difficult experience results in sin when we stop listening to and trusting God, and instead start listening to the devil's lies chiming with our own evil desires.

10. ... When we pray, "Lead us..." how are we being humble? We recognise that we need God's help and protection. The evil one is at work in the world, especially against Christians, and at all times we can be led astray and fall. We understand our own weakness—our gullibility, forgetfulness and resistance to God's word—and we're aware of the devil's plans and strategies. It's another plea for God to provide what we lack. We must demolish any sense of self-security. (See 1 Corinthians 10 v 12.) **And when we pray, "Deliver us..." what are we to be confident about?** This prayer recognises that God is sovereign over the evil one, seen in what Jesus achieved on the cross (Hebrews 2 v 14). We're not asking him for something that is only a possibility, but something he will do. The One who ensured the defeat of Satan at the cost of the crucifixion of his Son is not going to leave us unequipped to endure in hard times so that we can't avoid falling into sin and the trap of the devil. (See 1 Corinthians 10 v 13.)

11. APPLY: How do we grow in both [humble dependence on God and confidence in him to provide what we need]? Though humility and confidence sound like opposites, they grow together. As we depend on God, we will experience his provision and grow in our confidence in him. As we grow in confidence in him, we depend upon him more and look to ourselves or others less. Allow people to share, perhaps from their own experience, what helps this growth process.

4 Hebrews 10 v 19-22; 4 v 14-16
THROUGH THE SON: PRAYING CONFIDENTLY

THE BIG IDEA
Through Jesus, our perfect sacrifice for sins and our sympathetic high priest, we can approach God with confidence that he will meet our needs.

SUMMARY
The truth that God is our perfect Father in heaven shapes how his people pray. We've seen that those who humble themselves will be justified, and Jesus teaches us to ask for, among other things, forgiveness. But the problem of Isaiah 59 v 2—"your sins have hidden [God's] face from you, so that he will not hear"—has not yet been explicitly answered.

This session looks at that answer: Jesus' ministry. Jesus fulfilled two important features of Old Testament Israel's national life and religion: the sacrifices and the high priest. Jesus our sacrifice "bore" our sin—he was punished by God as a sinner, carrying all sin. Jesus our high priest now intercedes for his people before God. Our sinless high priest is also our human brother; he has experienced the same temptations as us.

In Christ, there is no longer any reason to fear God, or doubt that he hears us or try to cover up when we talk to him. But only followers of Jesus can come to God with this confidence that our prayers will connect with our heavenly Father. This session challenges us to do just that.

OPTIONAL EXTRA
(1) If your group have little Bible knowledge, show a plan, model or online virtual tour of the tabernacle/Jerusalem Temple, and explain about the Most Holy Place and the curtain, mentioned in Hebrews 10 v 19, 20. (2) Who would you go to for help? Tell people that they need help with several tasks. For each task provide a list of three possible helpers (those known to the group or celebrities or fictional characters) and get people to choose one. Helpers should include those who are unqualified, super-qualified, and somewhere between; and people who are approachable or intimidating. Examples: get fit—choose from zumba-mum Zoe, marathon-addict Mike or couch-potato Chris; cook dinner—choose from Justin Bieber, Gordon Ramsey or Britain's favourite veteran baking expert, Mary Berry. Some will choose someone for their expertise; others will be swayed by people's approachability. (Links with Q12)

GUIDANCE FOR QUESTIONS
1. Why do people think that God might listen to them and answer when they pray? Recap what we learned about the prayer of religious hypocrites and pagans in Session 2.

• **How confident are they about this, do you think?**

2. What can Christians do, and why can we do that (v 19-20)? We can enter the Most Holy Place—the presence of God—because Jesus died to open a way through the barrier between us and God, caused by our sin and symbolised here by the temple curtain.

• **Why is this so remarkable?** (If your group have little Bible knowledge, remind them of Isaiah 59 v 2; see p7 in Study Guide.) From the moment when Adam and Eve were expelled from Eden (Genesis 3 v 23-24)—where God used to meet them (v 8)—until the moment when the temple curtain was torn apart as Jesus was dying on the cross (Mark 15 v 38), no one could come to God with confidence that they would be accepted and not destroyed. And that's still the case for everyone born into this world… unless the way to God is opened for them by the blood of Christ, as they put their faith in him. No other religion gives certainty that sinful people will be welcomed by the perfectly just and holy God.

3. Explain what the blood of Jesus has done for his people. See Hebrews 9 v 28 and 2 Corinthians 5 v 21. This is an opportunity for people to try explaining the heart of the Christian good news. Jesus died as a sacrifice that would take away the sins of many people. He had no sin, but he "bore" our sin—he was treated by God as a sinner, carrying all the sins of the world. As a result of his death, we can be united by faith to the risen Jesus and receive his righteousness. So God treats us as he treats Jesus—he accepts us, welcomes us into his presence and listens to us.

4. In light of these truths, what should Christians do (Hebrews 10 v 22)? We should "draw near to God"—we should talk to him. We should do this because Christians, alone of all people, can. And how should we do this? With sincerity and full assurance; we no longer need to cover up or to impress God, because we are confident that he will accept us in Christ.

5. What does it mean to draw near to God with a "sincere heart"? (What is the opposite of a sincere heart?) Sincerity means being able to show and express our true feelings. The opposite is trying to cover up our true selves and present a version which we hope will impress or be liked.

6. What can we be sure of when we have faith in Christ? We can be confident that however we feel about ourselves, or whatever we have done, in Christ we are acceptable to God and loved by him.

EXPLORE MORE [Philippians 3 v 2-9]
What were the reasons why Paul was once confident that he was righteous before God? His circumcision at eight days old, his nation (Israel), his tribe (Benjamin), his ethnic purity (a Hebrew of Hebrews), his education and status (a Pharisee), his commitment to Judaism (persecuting the church) and his devotion to the law (faultless).
What kind of things might we add to our own list? Let people share what they would be tempted to add.
How does Paul now view these reasons for his past confidence (v 7-8)? As garbage!
What are the signs that someone is boasting in (relying on) Christ? Their righteousness before God and their confidence to approach him come only from Christ; and so knowing him becomes more important than anything else in their life. **Or that someone has gone back to putting confidence in things that people do?** Christ becomes less central to what they do and say. Other things (see the first two Explore More questions) become more important.

7. APPLY: Why do you think we

Christians sometimes don't do what we wonderfully can do—that is, draw near to God? Encourage people to share from their own experience. Answers might include laziness, busyness, everything going well (all indicating that we are self-sufficient and see no need of God's help offered freely to us in Christ); or fear, feeling unworthy and undeserving, too wrapped up in our own problems (all indicating that we don't trust that God will find us acceptable in Christ).

8. APPLY: People around us may have an unfounded confidence that if they pray to God he will hear and answer them. What should we be saying to them? Discuss how people might approach talking to non-Christians about the only sure foundation for confidence that God will hear us when we pray to him. Isaiah 59 v 2 might be a good passage to share, followed by the passages mentioned in the answer to Q3—2 Corinthians 5 v 21 and Hebrews 9 v 28—and finally the passage for this session: Hebrews 10 v 19-22.

9. Jesus is the sacrifice for sin, but what other role does he carry out for his people (v 14; see also 10 v 21)? Jesus is our great high priest. You might need to explain that in Old Testament Israel the high priest was the sole person appointed to enter God's presence in the Most Holy Place of the Tent of Meeting (later, the temple) once a year to make atonement for the whole nation. That meant paying for all the nation's wrongdoing by means of the required sacrifice to secure reconciliation with God.
Note: Jesus is the fulfilment of many aspects of Old Testament Israel's national life and religion: the sacrifices and the high priest—as well as the temple, the Passover lamb, the king and the prophets. All these point to

Jesus and what he came to do.
- **See Hebrews 5 v 1-2 and 7 v 25: What are the responsibilities of this role (find three)?** (1) The high priest represents people before God (5 v 1) and intercedes for them (7 v 25)—he is a mediator. (2) He offers gifts and sacrifices to God on the people's behalf (5 v 1). (3) He teaches and corrects those who are ignorant and going astray (v 2).

- **See Hebrews 7 v 23-27: How is Jesus far better than the Jewish priests in Jerusalem were (find two things)?** (1) Jesus lives for ever, so he is a permanent priest, always able to save and to intercede for those who come to God through him (v 24-25). (2) Jesus is pure and blameless—he didn't need to offer a sacrifice for his own sins; so his sacrifice of himself for sins was effective "once for all" (v 27).

10. Adding to what we have just learned about Jesus our high priest, Hebrews 4 v 14-16 gives us another reason for confidence to approach God. What is that? Though Jesus is eternal, pure and blameless, he has also "been tempted in every way, just as we are—yet he did not sin" (v 15). So he understands what it's like to be us, with weak bodies, powerful physical drives, and minds affected by hunger, tiredness, pain or distress. That's why we can have confidence to come to him and ask for his grace to help us through these tough experiences. We know he will help us because he won't belittle us or minimise our experiences, and because the goal of all his life and work was to make us like himself—holy, pure and blameless.

11. APPLY: What light does Hebrews 4 v 14-16 shed on what we should pray for? We need to pray about our weaknesses and the temptations we face, asking God for his mercy and grace to help us whenever we face these kinds of things.

- **What should we expect to happen as a result?** We should be confident of receiving the help that we ask for. We need never think that temptation is overwhelming and so sin is inevitable.

12. APPLY: What inadequate views of Jesus do we often have, and how do they affect our confidence to ask for God's help when we are weak and tempted? This is a further opportunity (see also Q7) to discuss how our view of Christ affects our prayers. If we view Christ as only divine—untouched by temptation and unaware of how human weakness feels—we will have no confidence that he understands our weakness. We'll avoid asking him for help in temptation, much as we might avoid sharing with an intimidatingly competent colleague or friend about our struggles. Or if we view Christ as merely human like ourselves, we'll have no confidence that he can help us, and that will undermine our desire to pray to him about these things, in the same way that it would be pointless to seek help with an exercise plan from a fellow couch-potato.

16ᵗʰ April

5 John 15 v 1-17
THROUGH THE SON: PRAYING DEPENDENTLY

THE BIG IDEA
When we remain in Jesus, our wishes and requests reflect his concerns and purposes; and it's in this context that he's promised we will be given whatever we ask for in prayer.

SUMMARY
Jesus, our once-for-all sacrifice and sympathetic high priest, has overcome the problem of our sin. Despite our sin, through faith in him we can confidently approach our heavenly Father. But many professing Christians think that once Jesus has saved them, the job's done.

In John 15 Jesus shows it's not enough to view him as some divine lifeguard who plucks us out of the water to send us on our way again. If we don't remain in Jesus, the true vine—if his words don't stay in us and his fruit doesn't keep growing in our lives—we are dead branches, which proves we were never saved. He's not only the way to God but the life.

To those who remain in him, Jesus promises that whatever we wish, and whatever we ask for in his name, will be done or given. These words have led some to make wild requests and far-fetched claims, often involving very worldly prosperity, success and power. This session helps us understand exactly what Jesus is saying here about the prayers that God promises to answer.

We're challenged to ask ourselves: Do our wishes come from Jesus' words in us or from something else? Are we really praying for things in Jesus' name? Are we even asking him for anything? Understanding what remaining in Christ means will help us answer these questions.

OPTIONAL EXTRA
Find *Still Life* by Sam Taylor-Wood online: a 4-minute time-lapse film of a bowl of fruit decaying. Before showing it, offer people some fresh, ripe fruit, and ask them what they think of it. After the film, discuss why the fruit decays (because it is cut off from the tree), and the difference between the fruit you offered and the mouldy fruit at the end of the film (no difference—it's just a matter of time until it all looks the same). (Links with Q2 and 3.)

GUIDANCE FOR QUESTIONS
1. If you could ask God for anything, what would you ask for? This question (linking with John 15 v 7 and 16) reveals the desires of our hearts. Even if we don't share the answer publicly, it tells us something about ourselves.

2. How does Jesus describe the relationship between himself and his true disciples? He is the vine and we are the branches (v 5a). He is the source of everything we need, and without him we are not only useless but dead.

- **Why is his picture so helpful?** It shows:
- how essential our relationship with Jesus is—without him we are dead branches.
- how we continually need him to provide for us what we need.
- our permanent unity with Christ—he's

not just our way into God's kingdom but foundational to the whole of our lives, here and in eternity.
• the outcome of a life united to Jesus—fruitfulness.

Compare these truths with popular ideas in churches about the relationship between Jesus and his people (see Summary above).

3. ... Jesus' words here help us know who are his true disciples. What's the key sign and what does it reveal about a person? The key sign is fruitfulness. Those who are not fruitful are cut off by the Father (v 2a); they prove that they are not united to Jesus (v 4); and are therefore "thrown into the fire and burned" (v 6).

• **How can we explain how some branches come to be dead?** Jesus and other New Testament writers often warn about those who self-identify as followers of Christ and believe themselves to be saved, but are not (e.g. Matthew 7 v 21-23; Titus 1 v 16; 1 John 2 v 4).

4. How does verse 8 show what it means to bear fruit? "Fruit" here is what shows that we are disciples of Christ. It involves living godly, Christ-like lives (e.g. Ephesians 5 v 8-10), but also speaking words—the gospel (e.g. Colossians 1 v 3-6). **And how is that different from simply being a nice or decent person?**
• Niceness and decency are not Christ-likeness. We can be nice and decent because of cultural pressure, or because it is the best way to a quiet life, or to manipulate others.
• Niceness and decency can be opposite to godliness; e.g. we may fail to speak truthfully in order to be seen as nice.

• Niceness and decency don't point people to Christ. That requires Christ-like deeds and gospel words.

5. The word "remain" can also be translated as continue, endure, or stay. What does remaining in Christ involve in practice?
• **v 7a:** His words remaining in us.

• **What does John mean by Christ's word(s)? See verse 3.** The word that Christ has spoken to them has made them "clean". It's the gospel. See also John 1 v 12-13; 3 v 16-18; 8 v 24.

• **v 9, then v 10, then v 12-13:** Remaining in his love (v 9), which is also part of his words remaining in us (v 10), and which shows itself when we love others as Christ has loved us (v 12). The words "remain", "stay" and "continue" suggest a settled and permanent state; the word "endure" suggests continuing in the face of difficulty. So true disciples of Christ are those whose settled and permanent way of life is to follow Christ's words and show his love, and who persevere in that even when it's tough.

6. APPLY: What's the warning here if we are not remaining in Christ and producing fruit (v 6), and how should this guide our prayers, do you think? The warning is that we don't belong to Christ and will be condemned at the judgment (compare Matthew 13 v 40-42). Our prayers, shaped by our branch-like dependence on Christ our Vine, will thank God for Christ, trust in Christ for all we hope for, and look to him for all we need; and we'll seek always to remain in him: to listen to his words, show his love and produce fruit that glorifies him.

• **What real-life example of not remaining in Christ is taking place as Jesus speaks (see John 13 v 21-30)?** Judas is about to betray Jesus. Note that none of the other disciples suspected Judas' intentions (v 22, 29)—for three years he looked like a real branch—but ultimately his words and actions showed that he wasn't a disciple of Christ.

• **What's the uncomfortable truth if we are fruit-bearing branches (v 2), and how should this guide our prayers, do you think?** God prunes fruit-bearing branches to make them more fruitful. "Pruning" looks and feels painful but it's necessary to produce a healthy branch. Compare 1 Peter 1 v 6-7. If we understand this about painful experiences, we can keep rejoicing and thanking God for his work in our lives during those times, and ask him to help us trust that he is working for our good in these times ("Deliver us from the evil one"—Matthew 6 v 13).

• **What real-life example of pruning was about to take place (see John 13 v 36-38)?** Peter was about to discover he wasn't as brave in following Jesus as he believed he was. Perhaps we can see how Peter matured through suffering this bitter experience and then being wonderfully restored; it's harder to see this in our own difficult experiences, but just as true.

7. APPLY: How can we tell that someone (ourselves even) is in danger of "moving on" from Christ instead of remaining

in him? We lose our first love for Jesus. We may be enthusiastic about the Bible, church, theology, outreach, ministry, or even God—but mention Jesus little and lack the same sort of passion about him. Eventually we lose interest in God's word and God's people; we return to old sinful patterns or become taken up with new interests.

• **How can we help each other to remain in Jesus?** Jesus commands us to "remain in [him]" (John 15 v 4)—we are to be intentional about this, taking steps to ensure this happens. Share practical ways of doing this: reading, listening to, memorising and sharing his word; asking God's help to keep our eyes fixed on Jesus; putting ourselves where we'll be reminded of Jesus' work, grace and love for us by spending time and meeting regularly with God's people.

EXPLORE MORE [Mark 9 v 14-29]
How does the failure of the disciples here provide a negative illustration of Jesus' words in John 15? When the disciples fail to drive out the evil spirit, Jesus rebukes them for unbelief (Mark 4 v 19), and pinpoints their lack of prayer to explain their failure (v 29). Previously, Jesus had given them his authority to drive out impure (evil) spirits (6 v 7), so it seems that the disciples had lapsed into relying on their own authority and abilities. They were no longer depending on Jesus and so their actions were fruitless.

By contrast, how does the boy's father provide a positive illustration? The boy's father has no confidence in himself—not even in his ability to believe in Jesus. So he turns to Jesus for help to overcome his unbelief (v 24). And in that very moment, he shows belief in Jesus.

How is this at odds with much teaching

today about what it means to have faith in God? Many seem to believe that faith can only be a strong, unshakeable confidence that God will bring about a particular outcome (e.g. healing an illness), and any doubt about that outcome is unbelief. We can be confident of many things God has promised, but in many situations we don't know precisely what God wants to happen. This story should encourage us that when we lack confidence about anything— when we feel weak, confused, fearful or undeserving—we can still show true faith by recognising our weakness and turning to Jesus for help.

How can we make the same mistake as the disciples? Get people to share about ways in which they are tempted to rely on their own abilities and resources, rather than depending on Jesus. **And what is the sign that we are making that mistake?** See v 28-29—as with the disciples, what reveals our lack of dependence on Jesus is that we don't pray.

8. What does Jesus promise in verse 7? To whom? Jesus promises those who remain in him that they can ask for whatever they wish and they will receive it.

9. Verse 7 begins, "If you remain in me and my words remain in you…" How then should we understand "ask whatever you wish"? (Compare Psalm 37 v 4.) Since remaining in Jesus means that his words remain in us, his words must have an effect on us (see, for example, Ephesians 4 v 21-24). Our wishes and desires become identical with God's, so of course we can be confident that when we ask for those things, God will give them. Similarly, in Psalm 37 v 4 we see that if our delight or desire is God himself, that is what God will give us—more knowledge of him, deeper love for him, and

a closer relationship with him. It's crucial that we understand the context and condition ("If you remain in me and my words remain in you…") needed for the fulfilment of this promise ("… ask whatever you wish, and it will be done for you.").

10. In light of verse 8, what kinds of things will Christ's disciples wish and ask for, do you think? As the words of Jesus remain in us, we will long more and more to bear fruit that shows we are his disciples—to speak his words and show his love—and so bring glory to our Father. Discuss with your group whether people are actually asking for these things.

11. What does Jesus promise in verse 16? To whom? Jesus again promises—this time to those who bear fruit for him (the same people as those who remain in him, v 7-8)—that they will receive whatever they ask for in his name.

- **What does he mean by "ask in my name", do you think? (Look again at verses 9-17.)** To do something in someone's name is to represent them and all they stand for (e.g. writing a letter in the name of the company you work for). In verses 9-17, we see things that are of key importance to Jesus: his Father's love for himself, and his love for his disciples (v 9); his Father's commands and his commands (v 10); his joy in his disciples, and his disciples' complete joy (v 11); his love for his disciples reflected in their self-sacrificial love for others (v 12-14); his relationship with his disciples—they are no longer servants but friends (v 14-15); his goal for his disciples—to bear fruit that will last (v 16). We can be confident that if we ask God to bring about and grow these things, he will do them: we'll be asking in Jesus' name. Again, discuss whether as individuals or as a church anyone is asking for these things; if not, why not?

12. APPLY: Imagine someone tells you, based on Jesus' promises here, that they are asking God for the six-figure salary they want, and they are certain that he will give it to them. What would you say to them? This is an opprtunity to recap what has been learned in this session and for people to practise applying it to a real-life situation.

13. APPLY: How does this passage guide you:
- **to think more carefully about what you pray for?** Reflect again on how closely in line your prayers are with God's priorities.

- **to be more adventurous about what you pray for?** Challenge people to think of things that they can ask for with complete confidence because they come from God's words in them, and then to ask!

- **to be more thankful in your prayers?** Encourage people to re-read the passage and pick out things that they can thank God for.

6 Romans 8 v 9-30
BY THE SPIRIT: PRAYING IN WEAKNESS

THE BIG IDEA
In this world we will be weak, yet we can be confident because the Spirit helps us in many ways and intercedes for us when we don't know what to pray.

SUMMARY
We've seen how Christian prayer is shaped by the fact that we talk to our Father in heaven through Jesus Christ and his ministry. Now we turn to the role of the Holy Spirit in the unique, distinctive kind of prayer that only Christians can enjoy.

In Romans 8 Paul shows how Christians in one sense are no different from non-Christians: our bodies are now still subject to death. But because the Spirit lives in us, our experience of life here is transformed. He empowers us to fight against our sinful nature; saves from slavery to fear; assures us of our intimate child-parent relationship with God; and gives hope beyond the grave. In this "changed but not yet changed" state we reflect creation, which has been subjected by God to frustration and decay. Creation and Christians are characterised by groaning, not in despair, but in eager expectation of God's promised new creation.

Because of the Spirit in us, Christians react and pray differently in tough situations from those around—in sickness, struggles with sin, facing death and suffering for following Christ. We are not to be blindly optimistic and unreal about these things; and we needn't despair.

But the Spirit's help goes further. For now we are weak, and that means often "we do not know what we ought to pray for" (v 26). Wonderfully, the Spirit translates our wordless groanings into precise, God-honouring requests. Because of him, there is no situation where we cannot pray to God—not even when we cannot speak a single word to him!

OPTIONAL EXTRA
Discuss a moral dilemma with your group—you can find a range of these by searching for "ethical dilemmas" online, or to think about one famous problem, go to wikipedia.org and search for "Trolley problem". It's highly unlikely that everyone will agree about what to do, and even after discussion some may still have no idea of how they should act. Similarly, we shouldn't be surprised that at times we won't know what we ought to pray for (see Q9 and 11).

GUIDANCE FOR QUESTIONS
1. What are the main reasons why people don't pray, or give up praying, do you think? There are no right or wrong answers here. One reason, highlighted in this study, is our weakness, revealed in the fact that we don't know what to pray for.

2. In what way are followers of Jesus different from everyone else (v 9)? The Spirit of God/Christ lives in us. Paul is very definite about this—if we don't have the Spirit, we don't belong to Christ. (V 5-8 outline the difference the Spirit makes.)

3. In what way are followers of Jesus no different from anyone else (v 10)? Our bodies are subject to death because of sin. You can't tell the difference between a Christian and a non-Christian by looking at their physical bodies—both will weaken, age and decay in the same way.

• **What does this mean for our expectations about our life in this world?** Physically (and mentally, since our minds and bodies are interconnected) we are susceptible to illness and injury, and we're heading for the grave. Life in this world, even for Christians, is never going to be perfect.

4. How might this tempt us to live (v 12-13)? To live as though we have one life only, and here and now is all there is. It's described here as living "according to the flesh" (v 13)—pursuing what the flesh wants (indulging our passions, lusts and appetites) in hostility to God and his law (see v 5-8).

• **What will stop us from living like this?** By the Spirit we can "put to death the misdeeds of the body" (v 13). That is, God gives us the Spirit to empower us to stop living "according to the flesh"—i.e. according to what we want to do and not what God wants—when we seek his help.

5. Although a Christian's body is still subject to death, the Spirit does change our experience of life in this world. In what ways (v 14-16)? The Spirit "testifies with our spirit that we are God's children" (v 16). It is by the Spirit that we relate to God as our Father, or "Abba" (the nearest translation in English is "Daddy"). The Spirit changes our experience of life in this world from fear—of the future, of death and of God's judgment—to a child-parent intimacy with God.

• **How does the Spirit change our perspective on life in this world (v 11, 17)?** We have the promise that one day the Spirit will give life to our bodies. He will resurrect us, as Jesus Christ has been resurrected. Our physical weaknesses and struggles are temporary. Our future life of freedom from physical suffering is eternal and will soon come.

6. APPLY: All Christians have the Spirit (v 9). How does that make Christian prayer different from any other kind? (Review what we've learned about the Spirit's work in us and think about how that affects our praying.) Christians pray to "Abba". We are cherished children of our loving Father, and so we are welcome to come to him at any time. Our concerns are his as well. We can be confident of his delight in us. Because we are no longer slaves to fear (v 15), we don't need to cover up when we come to God, or seek to impress him, or try to bargain with him. Once again, "humble" and "confident" are the key words that describe real Christian prayer.

7. APPLY: This passage shows what Jesus' followers can and can't expect in this life. How does this guide our praying, for ourselves or others: • in sickness? Romans 8 is clear, first, that in this world our bodies are "subject to death because of sin" (v 10); and second, the Spirit will raise us with eternal and truly living bodies in the future (v 11). So we shouldn't be surprised by sickness, or automatically expect healing if we pray for it. We can pray about sickness (see Philippians 4 v 6), but there's no promise that all or even most Christians will be healed.

• **when facing death?** A Christian's death is transformed by the Spirit because, like Christ, we will be resurrected (v 11). Slavery to fear has been taken away (v 15), since death no longer means meeting our Judge, but our Father. So a Christian facing death can pray, by the help of the Spirit, with thanksgiving and joy.

• **when struggling to overcome a particular sin?** We are promised that by the Spirit we can put to death the misdeeds of the body (v 13). The Spirit doesn't end our struggle in a knockout blow against sin, but rather, equips us to persevere in the struggle (see Galatians 5 v 16-25). We need to pray for his help and we can be confident of getting it.

• **when feeling far from God?** The Spirit "testifies with our spirit that we are God's children" and through him we can come to God as our "Abba" (v 15-16). So we can ask God for that testimony in our spirit, and come to God as our Father— even when we feel far from him. When a specific sin makes us feel distant, 1 John 1 v 9 and 2 v 1 are helpful verses on which to base our prayers. But when we don't know why we feel distant, we can remind ourselves that we are loved regardless of how we feel (see Romans 5 v 8).

• **when suffering for following Jesus Christ?** We share in Christ's sufferings, which also means we are heirs of God and will share in Christ's glory (v 17). The Spirit in us is the guarantee of this inheritance (Ephesians 1 v 14). When suffering for Christ, we can still rejoice when we pray.

8. In what way do verses 18-21 reflect what we have already learned in verses 9-11? As in Romans 8 v 9-11, there is a contrast between life in this world and in the future new creation. But the focus has moved from the experience of individual Christians to the whole of creation, which now is frustrated and decaying, but one day will be liberated (v 20-21).

• **What does this mean for our expectations about this world?** It is not now as it should be, and one day will be. We cannot make a perfect world now, but we should be in no doubt that God will make a perfect world in the future.

⌄

• **Paul describes the "groaning" of creation, and of Jesus' followers (v 22-23). What does this groaning express?** The key phrase is "pains of childbirth". Childbirth is painful, but hopeful—the pain signals the arrival of new life. The pain of living in this frustrated, decaying world signals the coming of the new creation. The groaning expresses expectancy. Christians are eager for the new creation because we have "the firstfruits of the Spirit" (v 23)—a partial experience now (e.g. forgiveness, God's fatherhood, fellowship with other Christians) of what the new creation will be like.

• **How is it different from the groaning we might hear from people around us?** Non-Christians have no future hope by which they can understand that the suffering of life in this world is temporary and brief; they can only groan in pain and despair.

9. How does our weakness show itself (v 26)? "We do not know what we ought to pray for." Part of our weakness is that we cannot fully know God's mind; and, at times, God's will can seem not only mysterious but contradictory. On one hand, we know that evil and suffering are not the goal for which God made us or creation; groaning is a right response to present sufferings. On the other hand, Christian suffering—like everything else—is under God's sovereignty, just as Christ's suffering was, and just as the frustration and decay of creation also are: creation has been subjected to these things by God (v 20). We can see how God uses evil for good (e.g. the cross), and maturing in faith includes increasingly understanding that God works in all things. But in specific situations we often don't know which of possible outcomes God wants. For example, where Christians are being persecuted, what does God want to happen? Should we pray for an end to persecution? Or for protection, escape or rescue from persecution? Or for courage to face martyrdom? "We do not know what we ought to pray for."

Another part of our weakness is that because we were made for a life that we don't yet have, pain, frustration and other evils of now cause us anguish, compounded by not knowing exactly how God is working out his plan. Even knowing that God works everything for good, we may be overwhelmed with distress, guilt, doubts, etc. Should we pray in line with what we know is true or with how we feel? Should we cry out like David, "Why have you forsaken me?" (Psalm 22 v 1)? Or declare like Jesus, "Not my will, but yours be done" (Luke 22 v 42)? We feel caught between praying insincerely and unbelievingly. Again, "we do not know what we ought to pray for".

• **How does the Spirit help us (v 26-27)?** He "intercedes for us…" (v 26, 27). He talks to God on our behalf. Our prayers aren't like press statements—we needn't fret over the precise words: the Holy Spirit sorts all that out. He intercedes "through wordless groans" (v 26). John Piper points out that these groans are not his, but

ours. "[The Spirit] moves powerfully in our hearts to create groanings—his groanings experienced as our groanings—which are based on two things: (1) a deep desire … that Christ be magnified in our lives, and (2) a weakness that leaves us baffled … as to how this is going to happen." (John Piper: "The Spirit Helps Us in Our Weakness, Part 2"; www.desiringgod.org/sermons) When God "searches our hearts", where we groan wordlessly, he hears "the mind of the Spirit"—our groanings translated into precise, God-honouring requests. And the Spirit prays "in accordance with the will of God" (v 27). We can be sure that praying when we don't know what to pray for will not result in a prayer against God's will.

10. In outline, what will the Spirit ask God for on our behalf (v 27-30)? These verses reveal that God's "purpose" and our "good" (v 28) are that we are "conformed to the image of his Son"—that we become like Jesus (v 29). So although we won't know precisely how the Spirit translates our wordless groanings, we can be confident that he asks the Father for whatever is needed to make us more like Christ.

11. APPLY: Think of situations in which Christians don't know what to pray for (perhaps one you face right now). If necessary, use the "persecuted Christians" scenario from Q9. **In each situation: • even so, what should you still do?** Keep praying—not knowing what to pray for is not a reason to give up. **• what can you be confident about?** If you long for God's will to be done, but have no idea what to ask for to achieve that, the Spirit will make a specific request on your behalf that God will be pleased to answer. **• what do you now know you can pray for?** We can confidently ask God to use a situation to make us more like Christ, even if we do not know exactly how that will happen.

• **How will the promise that the Spirit helps us in our weakness comfort us in times of distress?** There is no situation where we cannot pray to God—not even when we are completely unable to speak a single word to him. If there is a wordless groan in our hearts, the Spirit will turn that into a prayer more eloquent and God-honouring than any words we can say.

EXPLORE MORE [Ephesians 6 v 10-20]
How could you summarise the armour of God in one or two words? It's the gospel—the message of salvation through Jesus Christ.
Prayer is part of defending ourselves against the devil (v 18). Who are we to pray for, when and how? *Who:* for "all the Lord's people". *When:* "on all occasions". *How:* "in the Spirit".
What does "pray in the Spirit" (v 18) mean, do you think? (See v 17.) The other reference to the Spirit here tells us that God's word is "the sword of the Spirit". This suggests that praying "in the Spirit" means praying in line with God's word and God's priorities, purposes and ways revealed there. Praying shaped by the gospel is powerful, devil-destroying prayer.
Look at Paul's situation when he wrote this letter (v 20; see also 3 v 1 and 4 v 1). What would most of us want people to pray for us in this situation? Probably to be freed from the chains.
How is Paul's prayer request for himself (v 19-20) shaped by his understanding of how Christians resist the devil? We resist the devil through the gospel. So Paul wants Christians to pray that he will be helped to fearlessly declare the gospel.

7 1 Corinthians 14 v 1–25
BY THE SPIRIT: PRAYING TO SERVE

THE BIG IDEA

The Spirit equips Christians for the common good of the church, and so when we meet together, we pray not only to speak to God but to serve others by building them up.

SUMMARY

At first glance the passage looked at in this final session may not seem to say much about prayer. Paul compares two gifts of the Spirit—prophecy and speaking in tongues. The context is how Christians should act as a body: in unity, interdependence and love. As he gives instructions about church meetings, Paul urges the Corinthian Christians to value and seek the gift of prophecy over speaking in tongues because of its intelligibility—its use will build up fellow Christians and convict unbelievers of God's truth.

A close look at these verses shows that speaking in tongues is actually praying: "Anyone who speaks in a tongue does not speak to people but to God" (v 2). But Paul doesn't commend speaking to God when the words used are unintelligible to everyone around. He is teaching that public prayer should not only be about speaking to God; like every other part of a church meeting, our praying is to communicate God's truth so that Christians can be built up in their faith and unbelievers convicted and brought to repentance.

This final session challenges us first to think about whether we ever pray publicly (defined in its widest sense), and second, to think about how to do that in a way

that will be clear, faithful to God's truth and helpful for others. Real prayer not only connects each of us with our Father in heaven, but can also be the means by which God transforms other lives, growing and building up the whole body of Christ's people.

OPTIONAL EXTRA

Give your group one or more examples of unintelligible English. There are plenty of examples on the Plain English Campaign website (see winners of their "Golden Bull" awards). You could discuss how unintelligibility makes people feel, or how unintelligible aspects of your church meetings might be. (Links with Q9 and 10.)

GUIDANCE FOR QUESTIONS

1. How important do you think it is for Christians to pray publicly when they meet together? Why do you think that? This question finds out what people think about whether and why Christians should pray together. As we'll see, the New Testament gives a surprising reason for doing so.

2. Read 1 Corinthians 12 v 4-11. What is the purpose of the gifts of the Spirit? The common good (v 7). Note how the term "gifts" (v 4) is equated with "service" (v 5) and "God's work" (v 6).

3. Read 1 Corinthians 12 v 27-31. What else do we learn about the Spirit's gifts? All Christians have a gift—all have a part in the body (v 27). But we don't all have the same gift (see also v 19). And no one has all the gifts, so each of us needs other Christians (see also v 21).

4. Paul tells the Corinthians, "Eagerly desire the greater gifts" (v 31). What does he mean by "greater gifts", do you think? (See also 14 v 1.) Paul ranks the first three gifts—apostles, prophets and teachers (12 v 28). In 14 v 1, prophecy is highlighted as an especially desirable gift of the Spirit. The "greater gifts" all involve communicating God's word. Compare Ephesians 4 v 11: the gifts that communicate God's word—including apostles, prophets and teachers—equip God's people to serve in the church.

Note: What exactly are the gifts of apostle and prophet? The God-given words of Old Testament prophets and New Testament apostles became the foundation of Christ's church; as such, these gifts are not given by the Spirit today (see Acts 1 v 21-22; 1 Corinthians 15 v 3-8; Ephesians 2 v 20; 3 v 4-6; 2 Peter 3 v 2, 15-16). New Testament prophecy seems to be different from Old Testament prophecy—e.g. it's tested by public evaluation (1 Corinthians 14 v 29) whereas OT prophets faced the death penalty for false prophecies (Deuteronomy 13 v 2-5; 18 v 20-22). OT prophecy became part of Scripture (Luke 24 v 27; Romans 1 v 2; 2 Peter 1 v 20), while NT prophecy involves speaking God's truth already revealed in Scripture. It may be seen perhaps in Spirit-empowered preaching; or it may be a more widely distributed gift employed in congregational sharing and testifying. Whatever the precise mode of prophesying might be, we can define prophecy as speaking truth from God.

Since we are not to expect the same gifts as each other, how can we all eagerly desire the greater gifts? The Spirit gives gifts to the body—the church. It's the context in which Paul always writes about gifts (see also Romans 12 v 4-8; Ephesians 4 v 7, 11-13). We are to eagerly desire the greater gifts for our church, rather than for ourselves.

5. What exactly is Paul talking about when he refers to speaking in a tongue (see v 2 and 13-15)? Make sure people look at the verses given, rather than discussing ideas they have heard. Verse 2 tells us that those who speak in a tongue speak to God, not to people. In verses 13-14 Paul switches from talking about speaking to praying in a tongue. Speaking in tongues, then, is a kind of praying.

6. What does prophesying achieve that speaking/praying in a tongue fails to achieve (v 4; see also v 23-25)? Prophecy "edifies" (builds up, strengthens) the church (v 4), and reveals truth from God to unbelievers (v 24-25). Speaking in tongues can't do this because the words spoken are unintelligible to other people.

- **Fill in the table … to contrast the effects of prophesying with those of speaking/praying in a tongue.** See top of next page.

- **Why do you think Paul says that for a church to desire the greater gifts (like prophecy) is to "follow the way of love" (v 1)?** Prophecy helps others—it edifies, encourages, strengthens, comforts and communicates (see table), allowing other believers to join in with our praise and thanksgiving to God, and unbelievers

EFFECTS OF PROPHESYING	EFFECTS OF SPEAKING IN A TONGUE
v 3: Strengthening, encouraging and comforting others	**v 2:** Speaking to God, not people
v 4: Edifies the church	**v 4:** Edifies only the speaker
v 16 (What should happen here?): Others can say "Amen" to (= they can join in with) your thanksgiving, i.e. it unites	**v 11:** Makes the hearer a foreigner to the speaker, i.e. it separates
v 19: It is intelligible—it communicates	**v 16:** It is unintelligible—it mystifies
v 24-25: It can lead unbelievers to see the truth about God	**v 23:** It can lead unbelievers to conclude that Christians are insane!

to come to know God.

Note: Some people find verse 22 confusing. It may help if you explain that a sign is something that directs you towards a place. Tongues direct non-Christians towards unbelief (see v 23), leaving them as unbelievers. Prophecy however directs non-Christians towards belief (see v 24).

7. What important purpose does praying in a tongue achieve (v 2)? (Make sure people look at the verse.) Someone who speaks in a tongue speaks to God.

• **Why is this not a good enough reason for Paul to commend praying in a tongue when Christians meet together?** Paul's focus from chapter 12 to 14 is on how the Spirit builds up the church through gifts and through love. He gives gifts "for the common good" (12 v 7), and the most excellent way of using those gifts—the only way that achieves their purpose—is to use them in love. So when we meet together, it's not enough to speak only to God when we pray. Even our praying needs to be understood by others so that it can build them up.

8. What insight does Paul's reasoning give us into the purpose of praying

publicly? As with everything else that we do when we meet, part of our purpose in praying together is to communicate the gospel. That means we need to think about who will hear our public praying.

• **In Matthew 6 v 5-6 Jesus instructs his followers to pray in secret. How does this fit with Paul's instructions here about praying in public?** The context of Matthew 6 v 5-6 is important: Jesus is teaching why and how his followers are to be different from the hypocrites who dominated Jewish religious life. Hypocrites only pray in public, seeking to impress others, rather than speak to God. So Jesus underlines the importance of his followers praying secretly, where only God can see. However, on other occasions Jesus prayed in public (e.g. Mark 6 v 41; Luke 10 v 21-23; John 17), and also told his disciples to do so (e.g. Luke 22 v 39-46).

9. APPLY: How will your [public] praying be affected by knowing that you are not only speaking to God but to edify fellow believers and witness to unbelievers? Allow people to share how this makes them think about their own prayers. We will want to be careful that we accurately reflect the teaching of Scripture in our prayers. But also, we will want to reflect—in a way that suits our individual personalities—our personal experience of being saved and changed by God, and now living a new life based on God's word.

Note: The definition of "public" prayer for Q9 (see Study Guide p46) aims to make this question as widely applicable as possible. If a professing Christian has never prayed with even only one other person, it would be good to discuss with them why, and talk about how to do that for the first time. One reason may be an erroneous view that prayer is a "priestly" act: something done by those seen as experts on behalf of so-called ordinary Christians. You should be able to point out that nowhere in the Bible passages we've looked at is there any foundation for such a view. Both Jesus and Paul make no distinction between Christians regarding the privilege of praying to our heavenly Father.

10. APPLY: In what ways might our prayers be unintelligible to those around us? Although we may not speak in tongues (other languages, see Dictionary on p44), our praying may be just as unintelligible because of Christian jargon or high-level language, or even because of mumbling, or quiet or rapid ways of speaking. It's more difficult for some than others to make themselves understandable to everyone (e.g. shy people). However, Paul has devoted most of chapter 14 to the issue of intelligibility in church meetings. Without it no one will be edified or convicted of the truth. This should spur us to make every effort to be more intelligible.

EXPLORE MORE [Acts 4 v 23-21]
Note: It's not clear whether these words

come from one prayer that everyone else verbally assented to, whether this one prayer captures the essence of others, or whether this is a summary gathered from many prayers. But clearly one or more of the Christians were praying aloud in a way that united all of them.

What situation propelled the Christians to pray (see v 1-4, 18-22)? Peter and John's return to their fellow Christians, having been arrested and imprisoned for preaching the gospel, and then released when the religious authorities could neither stop them nor decide how to punish them.

What was the theme of their praying (v 24-28)? God's sovereignty in the face of top-level human opposition.

What informed their praying?
v 25-26: Psalm 2. **v 27-28:** The Roman and Jewish plot carried out against Jesus.

What's surprising about their request? (How might we have prayed differently?) They asked for boldness to continue doing the very thing—preach God's word—for which Peter and John had just been persecuted; and for God to authenticate his word. We might have asked for the enemies of the gospel to disappear so we could carry on preaching without much need for boldness!

How did these Christians use their minds as they prayed (compare 1 Corinthians 14 v 14-15)? They reminded themselves of Scripture and applied it to their situation, so that their prayers were based on unseen reality (that God's sovereignty determines what happens), and not on what only appeared to be real (that ungodly worldly power controls what happens).

How can we see that people were edified by this prayer? After they prayed, they "spoke the word of God boldly" (v 31).

11. APPLY: How do our prayers sound when we pray with a mind informed by the gospel and enlightened by the Spirit? What things might we start praying for, or stop praying for? There have been several questions throughout this series highlighting how we might need to change the content of what we pray for in light of what we have learned from God's word (see Session 1, Q12; Session 4, Q12; Session 5, Q13; Session 6, Q6-7). Get the group to discuss how their praying has changed. If it hasn't changed, talk about why that might be, and what would help people.

Good Book Guides
for groups and individuals

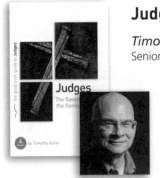

Judges: The flawed and the flawless

Timothy Keller
Senior Pastor, Redeemer Presbyterian Church, Manhattan

Welcome to a time when God's people were deeply flawed, often failing, and struggling to live in a world which worshipped other gods. Our world is not so different—we need Judges to equip us to live for God in our day, and remind us that he is a God of patience and mercy.
Also by Tim Keller: Romans 1–7; Romans 8–16; Galatians

Daniel: Staying strong in a hostile world

David Helm
Lead Pastor, Holy Trinity Church, Chicago

The first half of Daniel is well known and much loved. The second is little read and less understood! David Helm leads groups through the whole book, showing how the truths about God in the second half enabled Daniel and his friends—and will inspire us—to live faithful, courageous lives.

Esther: Royal rescue

Jane McNabb
Chair of the London Women's Convention

The experience of God's people in Esther's day helps us in those moments when we question God's sovereignty, his love, or his faithfulness. Their story reveals that despite appearances, God is in control, and he answers his people's prayers—often in most unexpected ways.

1 Corinthians 1–9: Challenging church

Mark Dever
Senior Pastor of Capitol Hill Baptist Church in Washington
DC and President of 9Marks Ministries

The church in Corinth was full of life, and
just as full of problems. As you read how Paul
challenges these Christians, you'll see how you
can contribute to your own church becoming truly
shaped by the gospel.
Also by Mark Dever: 1 Corinthians 10–16

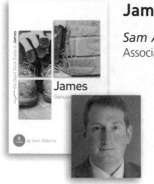

James: Genuine faith

Sam Allberry
Associate Minister, St Mary's Maidenhead, UK

Many Christians long for a deeper, more whole-
hearted Christian life. But what does that look like?
This deeply practical letter was written to show us,
and will reveal how to experience joy in hardships,
patience in suffering and whole heartedness in
how we speak, act and pray.
Also by Sam Allberry: Man of God / Biblical Manhood

1 Peter: Living well on the way home

Juan Sanchez
Preaching Pastor, High Pointe Baptist Church, Austin, Texas

The Christian life, lived well, is not easy—because
we don't belong in this world. Learn from Peter
how to journey on rather than retreat, and to do
so with joy and hope, rather than gritted teeth.

thegoodbook
COMPANY

God's Word For You

These expository guides can be read cover to cover, used daily for personal quiet times, or used to help you teach others. Trusted Bible teachers take you through these books of the Bible in an engaging and applied way. They all have accompanying Good Book Guides.

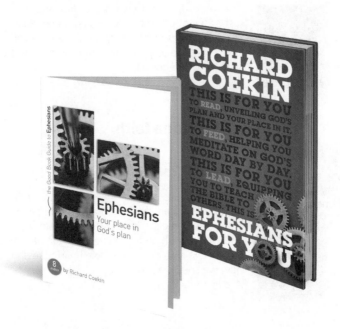

Ephesians For You
& Ephesians Good Book Guide

"Few are the commentaries that are simultaneously careful with the text, yet cast at the level of popular exposition— and Richard Coekin's is among the very best."

D.A. Carson

James For You
& James Good Book Guide

What is the difference between genuine and counterfeit faith? How do we know our faith is real? How can we know joy in trials, and patience in suffering? Sam Allberry unpacks the letter of James with typical perceptiveness, clarity, reality and humour.

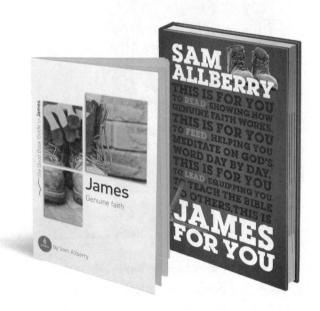

"Soundly doctrinal, eminently practical and beautifully devotional, this might just be the most accessible yet serious commentary on James available."

Russell Moore

MORE GOOD BOOKS
ABOUT PRAYER:

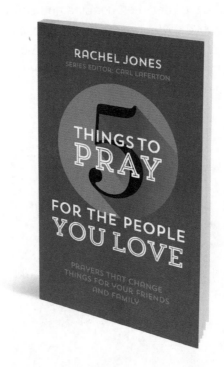

If we love our friends and family, we'll be praying for them. But often our prayers for them can feel shallow, repetitive and stuck in a rut.

That's where this little book will help: each section takes a passage of Scripture and suggests five things to pray for a person in your life, because when we pray in line with God's priorities as found in his word, our prayers are powerful—they really change things.

THEGOODBOOK.CO.UK/5THINGSLOVE

If we want God to be at work in our church, we pray. But so often our prayers for our church can feel shallow, repetitive and stuck in a rut.

That's where this little book will help: each section takes a passage of Scripture and suggests five things to pray for your church family, because when we pray in line with God's priorities as found in his word, our prayers are powerful—they really change things.

THEGOODBOOK.CO.UK/5THINGSCHURCH

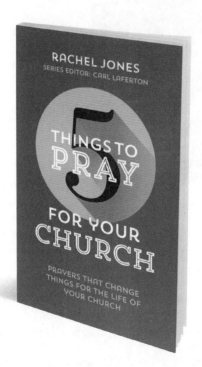

LIVE | GROW | KNOW

Live with Christ, Grow in Christ, Know more of Christ.

REBECCA MANLEY PIPPERT

Globally renowned speaker and author of *Stay Salt*

PART **1**

live

Explores what the Christian life is like.

Ever got to the end of running an evangelistic course and wondered: What next?

LiveGrowKnow is a series from globally renowned speaker Rebecca Manley Pippert, designed to help people continue their journey from enquirer to disciple to mature believer.

Part 1, Live, consists of five DVD-based sessions and is the perfect follow-up to an evangelistic course or event, or for anyone who wants to explore the Christian life more deeply.

PART **2**

grow

Explores how we
mature as Christians.

I'm a Christian… what next?
These studies show what
God's plan for our lives is,
and how we can get go-
ing and get growing in the
Christian life. For groups who
have done the LIVE course,
GROW is the follow-up; it
also works perfectly as a
stand-alone course.

PART **3**

know

Looks at core
doctrines of the faith.

Know looks at core
doctrines of the Christian
faith in an accessible and
applied way. The five
DVD-based sessions help
deepen understanding
on the trinity, creation,
fall, redemption and
Christ's return.

thegoodbook
COMPANY

Good Book Guides
The full range

Exodus: 8 Studies
Tim Chester
ISBN: 9781784980269

Judges: 6 Studies
Timothy Keller
ISBN: 9781908762887

Ruth: 4 Studies
Tim Chester
ISBN: 9781905564910

David: 6 Studies
Nathan Buttery
ISBN: 9781904889984

1 Samuel: 6 Studies
Tim Chester
ISBN: 9781909919594

2 Samuel: 6 Studies
Tim Chester
ISBN: 9781784982195

1 Kings 1–11: 8 Studies
James Hughes
ISBN: 9781907377976

Elijah: 5 Studies
Liam Goligher
ISBN: 9781909559240

Esther: 7 Studies
Jane McNabb
ISBN: 9781908317926

Psalms: 6 Studies
Tim Chester
ISBN: 9781904889960

Psalms: 7 Studies
Christopher Ash &
Alison Mitchell
ISBN: 9781904889960

Ezekiel: 6 Studies
Tim Chester
ISBN: 9781904889274

Daniel: 7 Studies
David Helm
ISBN: 9781910307328

Hosea: 8 Studies
Dan Wells
ISBN: 9781905564255

Jonah: 6 Studies
Stephen Witmer
ISBN: 9781907377433

Micah: 6 Studies
Stephen Um
ISBN: 9781909559738

Zechariah: 6 Studies
Tim Chester
ISBN: 9781904889267

Mark 1–8: 10 Studies
Tim Chester
ISBN: 9781904889281

Mark 9–16: 7 Studies
Tim Chester
ISBN: 9781904889519

Luke 1–12: 8 Studies
Mike McKinley
ISBN: 9781784980160

Luke 12–24: 8 Studies
Mike McKinley
ISBN: 9781784981174

Luke 22–24: 6 Studies
Mike McKinley
ISBN: 9781909559165

John: 7 Studies
Tim Chester
ISBN: 9781907377129

John 1–12: 8 Studies
Josh Moody
ISBN: 9781784982188

John 13–21: 8 Studies
Josh Moody
ISBN: 9781784983611

Acts 1–12: 8 Studies
R. Albert Mohler, Jr.
ISBN: 9781910307007

Acts 13–28: 8 Studies
R. Albert Mohler, Jr.
ISBN: 9781910307014

Romans 1–7: 7 Studies
Timothy Keller
ISBN: 9781908762924

Romans 8–16: 7 Studies
Timothy Keller
ISBN: 9781910307311

1 Corinthians 1–9:
7 Studies
Mark Dever
ISBN: 9781908317681

1 Corinthians 10–16:
8 Studies
Mark Dever & Carl Laferton
ISBN: 9781908317964

2 Corinthians:
7 Studies
Gary Millar
ISBN: 9781784983895

Galatians: 7 Studies
Timothy Keller
ISBN: 9781908762566

Ephesians: 10 Studies
Thabiti Anyabwile
ISBN: 9781907377099

Ephesians: 8 Studies
Richard Coekin
ISBN: 9781910307694

Philippians: 7 Studies
Steven J. Lawson
ISBN: 9781784981181

Colossians: 6 Studies
Mark Meynell
ISBN: 9781906334246

1 Thessalonians:
7 Studies
Mark Wallace
ISBN: 9781904889533

1&2 Timothy: 7 Studies
Phillip Jensen
ISBN: 9781784980191

Titus: 5 Studies
Tim Chester
ISBN: 9781909919631

Hebrews: 8 Studies
Justin Buzzard
ISBN: 9781906334420

James: 6 Studies
Sam Allberry
ISBN: 9781910307816

1 Peter: 6 Studies
Juan R. Sanchez
ISBN: 9781784980177

1 John: 7 Studies
Nathan Buttery
ISBN: 9781904889953

Revelation: 7 Studies
Tim Chester
ISBN: 9781910307021

TOPICAL

Man of God: 10 Studies
Anthony Bewes & Sam
Allberry
ISBN: 9781904889977

Biblical Womanhood:
10 Studies
Sarah Collins
ISBN: 9781907377532

The Apostles' Creed:
10 Studies
Tim Chester
ISBN: 9781905564415

**Promises Kept: Bible
Overview:** 9 Studies
Carl Laferton
ISBN: 9781908317933

The Reformation Solas
6 Studies
Jason Helopoulos
ISBN: 9781784981501

Contentment: 6 Studies
Anne Woodcock
ISBN: 9781905564668

Women of Faith:
8 Studies
Mary Davis
ISBN: 9781904889526

Meeting Jesus: 8 Studies
Jenna Kavonic
ISBN: 9781905564460

Heaven: 6 Studies
Andy Telfer
ISBN: 9781909919457

Mission: 7 Studies
Alan Purser
ISBN: 9781784983628

Making Work Work:
8 Studies
Marcus Nodder
ISBN: 9781908762894

The Holy Spirit: 8 Studies
Pete & Anne Woodcock
ISBN: 9781905564217

Experiencing God:
6 Studies
Tim Chester
ISBN: 9781906334437

Real Prayer: 7 Studies
Anne Woodcock
ISBN: 9781910307595

COMPANY

BIBLICAL | RELEVANT | ACCESSIBLE

At The Good Book Company, we are dedicated to helping Christians and local churches grow. We believe that God's growth process always starts with hearing clearly what he has said to us through his timeless word—the Bible.

Ever since we opened our doors in 1991, we have been striving to produce Bible-based resources that bring glory to God. We have grown to become an international provider of user-friendly resources to the Christian community, with believers of all backgrounds and denominations using our books, Bible studies, devotionals, evangelistic resources, and DVD-based courses.

We want to equip ordinary Christians to live for Christ day by day, and churches to grow in their knowledge of God, their love for one another, and the effectiveness of their outreach.

Call us for a discussion of your needs or visit one of our local websites for more information on the resources and services we provide.

Your friends at The Good Book Company

thegoodbook.com | thegoodbook.co.uk
thegoodbook.com.au | thegoodbook.co.nz
thegoodbook.co.in